THE ORIGINS OF THE CENTER

FOR HELLENIC STUDIES

THE
ORIGINS
OF THE
CENTER
FOR
HELLENIC
STUDIES

Eric N. Lindquist

PRINCETON UNIVERSITY PRESS

Copyright © 1990
by The Center for Hellenic Studies

Library of Congress Catalogue Card No. 90-82642
ISBN 0-691-03174-6

Printed in the United States of America
by Princeton University Press
at Princeton, New Jersey

FOREWORD

F OR NEARLY thirty years, I have served with great
pleasure on the administrative committee of the Center for Hellenic Studies in Washington, D.C. (Living across
the street from the center, I do not have to go very far to
attend its meetings.) Before the committee sits down to offi-
cial business, the fellows of the center usually join us for
cocktails, which always makes for an extremely pleasant occasion. The fellows are young scholars who come from all
over the world to spend a year in the quiet atmosphere of the
center, engaged in the study of ancient Greek civilization. I
am always impressed by their eagerness and their absorption
in their studies. For them, as indeed for many others who
have studied this ancient culture, the Greeks are alive still.
After these meetings I always come away with a renewed
confidence that the center is accomplishing the purposes for
which it was founded.

As this book relates, the establishment of the Center for
Hellenic Studies was complicated and protracted. In the
midst of our deliberations, I could not help but think some-
times of Odysseus' tortuous journey home from the Trojan
War. Our own journey also took ten years—from the first
conception to the dedication of the center's permanent buildings. At the same time, it was a fascinating experience. It all
started with a feeling that something should be done to advance the humanities, which seemed to me to be suffering
from serious neglect. Consultations with a variety of experts
yielded many exciting ideas, not all of them, unfortunately,

very practical. In the end—though I say this as a loyal graduate of Yale—it was Harvard's President Pusey who made what seemed to me the best proposal.

I remember vividly the lovely spring day in 1963 when we dedicated the center in front of members of the governing bodies of Harvard and other guests. The next day there was a better-publicized event, to which I alluded in the speech I delivered on the occasion. Astronaut Gordon Cooper was launched into space, which brought the nation a step closer to that greatest of human journeys, the voyage to the moon. A great deal has happened to all of us since that day. Some of those young scholars with whom I spoke in earlier years have become senior scholars, and venerable authorities in their fields. I am pleased that the center has been able to contribute to their scholarly development, and that it will continue to nourish the talents of their successors in the future.

PAUL MELLON

ACKNOWLEDGMENTS

I WROTE THIS BOOK while employed in the office of Paul Mellon. The project was suggested by Thomas H. Beddall, long-time Assistant to Mr. Mellon, who thought that the story of the origins of the Center for Hellenic Studies should be written while many of those who were there were still available to talk about it. I should like to thank Mr. Mellon and Mr. Beddall for their help and encouragement. Mr. Beddall submitted to an interview and commented in considerable detail on several drafts of the book. I should also like to acknowledge with the deepest appreciation a number of other individuals and organizations for assistance of various kinds. Lynn Page Whittaker provided expert editorial advice and sustained me through the project in countless ways. Nathan M. Pusey, President Emeritus of Harvard University, and Bernard M.W. Knox, Director Emeritus of the Center for Hellenic Studies, granted me interviews and commented helpfully on a draft of the book. Zeph Stewart, the current Director of the Center for Hellenic Studies, gave me generous access to the center's files and discussed the center with me at considerable length on several occasions. He also commented extensively on a draft of the book, saving me from a number of errors. Carroll J. Cavanagh, Principal Assistant to Mr. Mellon, read and commented on the text. Brenda Nowlan designed the frontispiece. Elizabeth Stanat, also of Mr. Mellon's office, did most of the work of assembling the appendix. Anne Keane of the Andrew W. Mellon Foundation was very helpful to me in my researches in the files of Old Dominion Foundation. At the Harvard University Archives, Harley Holden, Curator, and Kathleen A. Markees, Curatorial Associate, went beyond the call of duty in helping me with my researches in the papers of Nathan M. Pusey. I would also like to thank the staffs of the Manuscript Division of the Library of Congress and Manuscripts and Archives, Yale University Library for their assistance when I visited those repositories. I am grateful to the following people for their kind assistance in obtaining photographs: Beverly Carter, Administrative Assistant, Paul Mellon Collection; Richard E. Saito, Architectural Archivist, Martha Shears, Archives Assistant, Robin Van Fleet, Archives Technician, and Maygene Daniels, Chief, all of the Gallery Archives, National Gallery of Art; Robert A. Boyer, Director of Finance and Administration, Sullivan & Cromwell; Sarah Saville Shaffer, Assistant Director, Decatur House; Robin McElheny, Curatorial Associate for Visual Collections, Harvard University Archives; and Margaret N. Burri, Curator of Collections, the Historical Society of Washington, D.C.

INCE 1961 the Center for Hellenic Studies has offered a haven for young scholars of ancient Greek literature, history, and philosophy to spend a quiet year, free of distraction, to reflect and write. The center is located, somewhat improbably, on Whitehaven Street in Washington, D.C. It stands in what has been described as a "sylvan enclave," in a part of Washington that is heavily populated with foreign embassies. How the center got there is an interesting and instructive story. It was created at a time when the humanities, and especially the study of ancient Greek, seemed in serious decline, and in a city that was not known then as a center of culture and learning. It began as one idea and ended up—after many years of discussion—as something quite different. An account of the evolution of the center offers a case study of American philanthropy in action and also contributes to an understanding of the place of the humanities in national life.

THE STORY BEGINS with the philanthropist Paul Mellon, who initiated the train of events that led to the establishment of the center and has given it nearly all of the funds it has ever received. Paul Mellon's father was the Pittsburgh banker Andrew W. Mellon, who arrived in Washington, D.C. in 1921 to serve as secretary of the treasury, an office in which he continued for eleven years. Andrew Mel-

Paul Mellon in 1963

lon's tenure had important consequences for the city's (and the nation's) cultural life. Washington, he felt, lacked the cultural institutions that distinguished the other important capitals of the world. To help remedy this, in 1936 he presented to the American people his great collection of European and American paintings and sculpture to form the nucleus of a national collection, along with the promise of funds sufficient to construct a building to house it. The National Gallery of Art, the fruits of his generosity, opened in 1941, four years after his death.

Paul Mellon meanwhile had been educated at Choate School, Yale University, where he studied literature, Clare College, Cambridge, where he studied history, and, just before World War II, at St. John's College in Annapolis, Maryland, whose strict course of study in the liberal arts, required of all students, included the study of ancient Greek. He was thus thoroughly grounded in the humanities. Mellon settled on a farm in northern Virginia, close to Washington, in the 1930s and later acquired a house on Whitehaven Street. (As we shall see, the fact that the center was also established on Whitehaven Street was coincidental.) In Washington he was involved, among other things, in the National Gallery of Art, of which he served as trustee (1945–1985), president (1963–1978), and chairman (1979–1985). While president of the gallery, he and his sister, Ailsa Mellon Bruce, gave the gallery funds to construct a new building, which was completed in 1977. The East Building, as it was called, housed additional exhibition space and a new Center for Advanced Study in the Visual Arts, an institute for the scholarly study of art history.

Mellon also devoted a great deal of time to the work of several philanthropic foundations, including the A. W. Mellon Educational and Charitable Trust, which his father had established in Pittsburgh, and two foundations that he him-

3

self had established in New York City in the 1940s. These were Bollingen Foundation, whose chief activity was book publication, and Old Dominion Foundation (its offices located in New York but named after his adopted state of Virginia), a general-purpose foundation which supported programs in education, the arts, mental health, and conservation, among other things.

Bollingen and Old Dominion foundations were concerned, in the words of a report issued by the latter, with promoting the "general understanding of our cultural heritage"—Bollingen Foundation through its books and Old Dominion Foundation through its grants, especially to colleges and universities "to strengthen liberal arts teaching and the role of the humanities in the curriculum."[1] This emphasis reflected Mellon's own predilections, which seemed increasingly out of step with the times. National interest in the humanities—the classics, history, literature, and related subjects—was not very high and appeared to be declining.

First of all, there was the long-term decline—or even general disappearance—of traditional liberal arts education, in which the humanities, mainly in the form of the classics, played a central role. By the time Mellon attended St. John's College just before World War II, its curriculum, which was actually highly traditional, had become an innovation; it was even called the "New Program." Once, all educated persons had learned classical languages. Now, such knowledge was becoming rare. As a sign of the times, Yale abandoned its Latin requirement in 1931. Instead of liberal education, the elective system and vocational training came to prevail in American higher education. The humanities meanwhile became specialized concerns. Not all students studied the humanities; a few students (and fewer and fewer over time) "majored" in them. And the professional teachers of the humanities pursued scholarship that seemed increasingly esoteric, not necessarily because it was, but because the audience capable of comprehending it was shrinking. Since the humanities, especially the classics, were no longer studied widely in schools and universities, they had less and less to do with the formation of national culture.

By the 1950s the decline of the humanities was underlined further by the rise of science and technology. World War II, the Cold War that followed, the growth in the postwar period of a prosperous consumer society—all put scientific and technological advance at the forefront of national concern. The National Defense Education Act, passed in 1958, was the chief effort in the period to boost American education; it was concerned chiefly with scientific and technical education. Congress passed it in a state of alarm after the Soviets had launched the first space satellite, which appeared to be a grave threat to American security. (The act also encouraged foreign language study, but *modern* foreign languages.) In this atmosphere, the humanities seemed more and more neglected, a situation that seemed to some observers to be leading to a grave imbalance in national beliefs and values. The educational reformer Abraham Flexner complained that science "is . . . running away with our national culture."[2]

National neglect was reflected in the level of financial support the humanities received relative to the sciences. In a report on the state of the humanities in America, published in 1959, the literary scholar Howard Mumford Jones noted that the annual budget of the American Council of Learned Societies, then the chief organization for promoting humane learning in America, was only 1/280 of the 1958 proposed budget of the National Science Foundation. "We think too meanly of the humanities in this country," Jones lamented.[3] In those years, before the establishment of the National Endowment for the Humanities, the federal government gave little for the support of humane learning. According to Flexner, the private sector was not supportive either. He complained that "neither individual philanthropists nor the foundations have made any systematic effort to develop the humanities."[4]

Paul Mellon was one of those who deplored the decline of the humanities in American life, and he resolved in effect to take up Flexner's challenge. Bollingen and Old Dominion foundations were contributing already to support the humanities, but Mellon wished to do more. By 1953, he recalled later, he and some of his advisers had became interested in "formulating a special project which would act as a general stimulus to Humanistic thought and education."[5] He wanted to do something substantial and innovative. "The question is," Huntington Cairns, one of his associates, noted in April of that year, "what is the best way to do it."[6] Mellon's first idea was to use the balance of funds held by the A. W. Mellon Educational and Charitable Trust, a sum of $25 or $30 million. Soliciting ideas from others, he wrote A. Whitney Griswold, who had been his classmate at Yale and now was Yale's president, "we have an obligation and an opportunity to do something in a very creative way for the humanities and the arts, or perhaps even toward a beginning of a synthesis of humanities and sciences." Mellon asked for Griswold's advice and said that he had already spoken with others, including Flexner and Cairns. Their thinking, he wrote, ran to a new foundation or "some sort of Institute," such as the Institute for Advanced Study in Princeton, New Jersey, of which Flexner had been the first director.[7]

Nothing came immediately of these consultations, but a year or two later an idea for an institute proposed by Huntington Cairns began seriously to engage Mellon's attention.

Huntington Cairns about 1950

Cairns was a lawyer by profession who served from 1943 to 1965 as secretary, treasurer, and general counsel of the National Gallery of Art. He also served the Treasury Department for many years as a censor of imported literature. Cairns's interests, however, were not confined to the law. He was a man of wide learning and impressive energy, who be-friended many writers—including H. L. Mencken, Henry Miller, and Ezra Pound—and himself wrote or edited a number of books. During most of its existence he was a trustee of Bollingen Foundation, which published two of his books, a literature anthology entitled *The Limits of Art* (1948) and *The Collected Dialogues of Plato* (1961), which he edited with Edith Hamilton. For his erudition, Cairns was known among some of his friends "affectionately . . . as The Sage."[8] In October 1954 Cairns submitted to Mellon a memorandum proposing an institute he called the "Residence" as the best means to promote the cause of the humanities. Two further memoranda on the Residence followed in June 1955 and December 1956.[9]

Cairns modeled his Residence in part on such existing scholarly institutes as the Institute for Advanced Study, All Souls College at Oxford (he once referred to the Residence as "an Hellenic All Souls"[10]) and Dumbarton Oaks in Washington, D.C., an institute for Byzantine and pre-Columbian studies that was part of Harvard University. The Residence would house a small number of senior fellows with permanent tenure and an equal number of junior fellows with temporary appointments. It would be concerned with ancient Greek civilization initially—or Hellenism, as Cairns called it—although it might concern itself with other subjects in time. The Residence would be located in Washington, D.C., where the fellows would have access to Dumbarton Oaks and the Library of Congress.

The Residence may have resembled the Institute for Advanced Study or Dumbarton Oaks, but apparently Cairns was not interested in merely establishing another "ivory tower" scholarly institute. In a wider sense, the humanities could be advanced by promoting a larger role for them in national culture; in a narrower sense, they could be advanced by promoting the research of professional humanists. Cairns wanted to do both, but apparently the former more than the latter. In fact he disapproved rather strongly of academic scholarship as it was then practiced. What Cairns evidently wished to create was a mission rather than a scholarly retreat, with the ambition of influencing national life more broadly. The Residence might sponsor scholarship, but that was not to be its only concern; it should be "an enduring institution of wide influence . . . exerted towards the reassertion of humanism in the arts, in the academic world, and in the nation as a whole." Cairns even thought that the Residence might train men "to guide public affairs."

Cairns's ambitions were prompted by a more extreme view of the problem Mellon wished to remedy. Mellon thought that there was a disturbing neglect of the humanities in American society; Cairns feared that the fate of civilization was in the balance. Cairns told the poet and critic Sir Herbert Read that if the next generation did not embrace what he called Hellenism, "we are faced with re-barbarization." To prevent this re-barbarization was "the whole point of the Residence."[11] One critic of Cairns's views, Jacques Barzun, was to call them "apocalyptic."[12] The Residence, Cairns hoped, would help rescue the world from the "organized vulgarity" of popular entertainment and the modern philosophical and intellectual maladies which threatened to corrupt it irretrievably. He was interested in what he called Hellenism not as a field of academic research—not because it would yield a rich harvest of scholarly books and articles—but because of the "view of the world" which he thought Hellenism embodied, a view that had become essential to saving civilization. The whole undertaking, Barzun commented, "has all the aspects of founding a church rather than an intellectual enterprise."[13]

Cairns did not want the Residence to be affiliated with a university. He distrusted universities, admitting later that the Residence represented "an implied criticism" of them.[14] He held the universities at least partly accountable for the current plight of the humanities, blaming them for abandoning liberal education in favor of vocational training. Even those members of the universities who *were* concerned with the humanities, the professional humanists, did not seem to him to redeem the situation. " 'Classicism' in the Universities," he wrote to Read, "means pedantic scholarship, obscurantism, and no thought at all."[15] The Residence had to remain independent of university influence so that its mission would not be diluted. If anything, Cairns hoped that the Residence would influence higher education, perhaps bringing about significant curricular reform.

For that reason, apparently, Cairns prescribed that the Residence should be situated in Washington. Washington had several universities, but none of such prestige as seemed likely to overshadow the Residence or threaten its independence. There was yet another argument for locating the Residence in Washington. As the nation's capital, Washington was the place where the influence of the Residence could be brought to bear most effectively on public life. Cairns's wife, Florence Butler, who was also a student of Greek and champion of her husband's ideas, commented later that the Residence had to be situated in Washington not because of what Washington could give the Residence "but because of what the Residence can give Washington—direction." She continued, "Government officials are perplexed, and they know they are perplexed. Huntington has been approached by men on every level of government asking, not only for advice concerning what to read, but advice concerning what to do."[16]

However worthy its goals, the Residence was to be criticized rather severely. The scheme posed a number of difficulties. Perhaps the main one was its overall vagueness, which involved Cairns in some contradictions. In Cairns's description, the Residence would be part retreat and part mission, simultaneously sponsoring scholarship and spreading humanistic propaganda. But these aims were probably irreconcilable. The former required leisure and independence while the latter required direction and collaboration. The difficulty was complicated by the fact that the only people who knew Greek any longer, and the only people who comprehended what Cairns meant by Hellenism, were academic scholars, who seemed among the least likely to serve his purposes. It would be difficult to turn them into missionaries or proponents of what one critic called the proposal's "ideological line."[17] But Cairns never reconciled the various contradictions in his scheme and indeed seemed largely unaware of them. Nor did he ever outline any specific strategy for the Residence to carry out its grand mission. He never really said what precisely the Residence should do. In May 1959, five years after Cairns had first proposed his idea, Ernest Brooks, Jr., a trustee of Old Dominion Foundation, commented that it was "difficult for him to visualize exactly what sort of work would be done in the Residence."[18]

Finally, there was another matter that should be mentioned here: Cairns's own role once the Residence was established. He never commented on this directly, but it was believed widely that he hoped to play a part, probably a prominent one. In 1958 Thomas H. Beddall, an assistant to Mellon, noted that Cairns's participation in the Residence was "implicit."[19] Others even thought that Cairns wished to be its director.[20]

Mellon commented to Griswold in December 1956 that Cairns's proposal was in a "fuzzy . . . state"; it obviously needed more refining.[21] Still, he gave it some encouragement. The trustees of Old Dominion Foundation (which had taken over the project of advancing the humanities from the A. W. Mellon Educational and Charitable Trust of Pittsburgh) had endorsed the idea generally. In June 1955 the trustees' finance committee "approved in principle the establishment of a Residence . . . modeled somewhat in structure upon All Souls College" and indicated their willingness to give it substantial support. The initial establishment, they agreed, should be on the scale of Dumbarton Oaks, "but with a pledge of sufficient funds to enable it, if successful, to grow to the scale of the Institute for Advanced Study."[22] Evidently the foundation was preparing to do something ambitious.

ABOUT THIS TIME another important figure entered the story: Marie Beale, widow of Truxton Beale, a wealthy diplomat. Among other posts, Truxton Beale had served as envoy extraordinary and minister plenipotentiary to Greece in the early 1890s. The Beales owned Decatur House, in Lafayette Square across from the White House, and Mrs. Beale was for many years a prominent Washington hostess. During World War II she was active in war relief, particularly in Greece, and afterwards aided preservation efforts in Venice.[23]

It happened that Huntington Cairns was a confidant and intellectual adviser to Mrs. Beale. The flavor of their relationship can perhaps be gathered in a note she wrote him in March 1950. "I took your Anthology [probably *The Limits of*

Marie Beale

Art] with me to Tucson," she wrote, "for I had never had a
real 'whack' at it. It was a delight to me, and how I do wish
that I could read classic Greek! I congratulate you on having
gotten together a book that one will always keep at hand."[24]
Cairns also succeeded in interesting Mrs. Beale in his plans
for the Residence, although her associations with Greece

probably helped. She owned one of the few remaining un-developed tracts of land in Washington, located on White-haven Street and also contiguous to Dumbarton Oaks, which had been the estate of her friends Mr. and Mrs. Robert Woods Bliss before they gave it to Harvard. Whitehaven Street was a perfect location for what Cairns had in mind, and he might have been thinking of it when he proposed that the site of the Residence should be both secluded and accessible.[25] Cairns must have talked with Mrs. Beale about his plans, and in 1955 he indicated to Old Dominion Foundation that she might be interested in donating her property.[26]

Nothing was done right away, but the next year the pro-posal was revived and, apparently under Cairns's influence, an agreement was concluded. In the spring of 1956 formal negotiations began between Mrs. Beale's advisers and the foundation.[27] Mrs. Beale was planning a trip to Europe for the late spring and summer (which was to include a tour of the Greek islands). Since there seemed to be no great urgency, she was inclined to wait until her return before concluding the agreement; but in the end, possibly at Cairns's urging, she decided to make the arrangements before her departure. Al-though she wanted to make the property available to the foundation for immediate use, her advisers counseled her to retain an interest in it in case she needed to receive some fi-nancial benefit from it in the future. After various proposals were considered, the agreement concluded finally between Mrs. Beale and Old Dominion Foundation provided for the foundation's immediate possession, with an option to pur-chase the property for $500,000. If she should need money in the future, she could require the foundation to exercise its op-tion. If the foundation did not then agree to purchase the property, it would revert to her along with any improve-ments. This was agreed to just before she sailed for Europe on May 13. She also changed her will, adding a provision in which she devised the property to Old Dominion Foundation and forgave the purchase price (or the unpaid remainder) in the event that the foundation had exercised its option to purchase. In all cases her land was to be used, as her will prescribed, "exclusively for the establishment of an educational center in the field of Hellenic studies designed to rediscover the humanism of the Hellenic Greeks."[28] However, the foundation would be allowed to assign the land to another agency to carry out the purposes of the will. It was fortunate for the future of the center that the agreement was executed before Mrs. Beale went abroad, for she died suddenly in Zürich on June 11.

The foundation accepted the devise of the land toward the end of 1956.[29] The trustees hesitated a little because of the restrictiveness of the will's language; they were not certain they wanted to limit themselves to "the field of Hellenic studies." However, they were assured that acceptance of the devise would not *oblige* them to establish an educational center such as the will described. If the foundation decided not to establish an institute for Hellenic studies, it could always assign the property elsewhere or simply forfeit it without penalty to itself.[30] There may have been some hope, too, that the courts would allow a liberal interpretation of Mrs. Beale's intentions.

The foundation's acceptance of the devise did, however, introduce a new complication. Mrs. Beale's will included an unusual provision, which prescribed that if the foundation or its assignee did not establish an educational center in the field of Hellenic studies on the Whitehaven Street property, the land would go over to the State Department, along with the residue of her substantial estate. (In that case she wished property and money to be used to establish an international con-

In this photograph, taken in 1938, Whitehaven Street (below) runs into Massachusetts Avenue at bottom right. The British embassy is in the center of the photograph and the U.S. Naval Observatory and Observatory Circle at the upper left. The Beale property is at bottom center. Today, the administration building of the Center for Hellenic Studies stands approximately on the site of the large house in the middle of the property. The Tompkins House, the first home of the center, is the second house from the left on Whitehaven Street.

ference center or other suitable institution, partly as a memorial to Walker Beale, her husband's son by a previous marriage, who had died in battle in World War I.) If, however, Old Dominion Foundation proceeded to establish a center for Hellenic studies on the property, the residue of her estate would go to Harvard University, to establish a fund for scholarships.[31] The residue turned out to be a considerable sum, over $4 million. Harvard, as an Old Dominion Foundation trustee said, thus had "a substantial economic interest in the organization of a center to comply with the conditions of the will."[32]

In the late spring of 1958 a will construction case heard in the U.S. District Court for the District of Columbia resulted in the distribution to Harvard of the residue of Mrs. Beale's estate, but the U.S. attorney wanted the university to maintain the bequest in a separate fund so that it would be convenient for the government to recover it in the event that the Whitehaven Street property was ever forfeited to the State Department.[33] For now, the court declined to say what would happen to Harvard's bequest if an educational center in the field of Hellenic studies was not established on Whitehaven Street, but it reserved the right to rule on the matter in the future. Harvard's possession of the scholarship money, then, was not absolute. It depended now on Old Dominion Foundation.

As soon as the court had made its ruling, Harvard officials approached representatives of the foundation.[34] Their understanding of the situation was somewhat muddled—some apparently thought that there was already a center in being and that it was just a matter of keeping it going—but the overall situation as it touched the university was clear enough. For the foundation the complication meant another burden. In addition to considering the worth of the project itself, the trustees had now to consider the effects of their decisions on Harvard. If they wanted to improve the position of the humanities, they could not neglect the interests of one of the nation's major universities and centers of humane learning. John D. Barrett, vice-president and secretary of Old Dominion Foundation, argued that the complications of the will should not influence their opinions of the Residence, but that was not easy to do.[35] As one trustee pointed out in December

1959, "it would not be good if Harvard should lose its bequest and the Foundation blamed."[36]

The trustees could wash their hands of the whole problem by assigning the property to another agency, as the will allowed. That assignee could indeed be Harvard. But almost certainly an assignee would want money along with the Whitehaven Street property. In any case, then, the trustees would probably have to consider whether the "educational center" prescribed in Mrs. Beale's will (modeled or not modeled on Cairns's Residence) was an idea worth the substantial investment it would probably require.

MEANWHILE, the Old Dominion trustees had made other preparations in case they decided in favor of an institute. In 1956, before the acceptance of the devise, the trustees acquired from Harvard a parcel of land adjoining the Beale property to ensure that the institute would have enough room.[37] The next year Mellon acquired a second house on Whitehaven Street, known as the Tompkins House, for its eventual use. Progress was slow, however, and by June 1958 Mellon had begun to worry that the foundation might lose the Beale property through inaction. The will had not prescribed how much time the foundation had to establish a center, or at what point it would forfeit the Whitehaven Street property to the State Department. The trustees sought the advice of Ezekiel G. Stoddard, a Washington attorney, who submitted a lengthy memorandum on the matter in the fall of 1958. Stoddard suggested in general terms that the foundation had about five years to establish a center such as Mrs. Beale had prescribed. In the meantime, as long as the foundation made some progress with its plans and did not appear to be abandoning the project, he thought the trustees probably did not have to be too anxious.[38] (It is interesting to note in retrospect that the Center for Hellenic Studies was dedicated almost exactly five years after the court's 1958 ruling on Mrs. Beale's will, so it was probably just as well that the foundation began to give the center greater attention at the end of 1958.)

By the time Stoddard reported, Mellon had taken another important step, appointing in August 1958 a committee of representatives of Old Dominion Foundation to examine the whole idea of the Residence and recommend a course of action.[39] The committee, known as the committee for the humanities, consisted of three foundation trustees, Ernest Brooks, Jr., Adolph W. Schmidt, and Stoddard M. Stevens, with Thomas Beddall serving as recording secretary. Brooks was president of the foundation. Schmidt was a businessman involved in Mellon banking interests in Pittsburgh. In addition to being a trustee of Old Dominion Foundation, he was president and trustee of the A. W. Mellon Educational and Charitable Trust in that city. Stevens, a long-time partner in the Wall Street law firm of Sullivan and Cromwell, was Mellon's lawyer and probably his most trusted adviser. Although he had become a trustee of Old Dominion Foundation only recently (in May 1958), he was to be the most forceful and influential member of the committee for the humanities.[40]

Significantly, none of the members of the committee was well acquainted with Cairns's ideas or had had anything to do with their formulation. Although the Residence was to serve as the starting point of discussion, Mellon wanted a fresh perspective on the whole question.[41] The committee was to proceed with all deliberation. The elements of a plan were available, but the trustees did not wish to rush into anything. The committee's brief was to consider the entire problem, beginning with the advisability of establishing the Residence or similar institute in the first place. In September 1958, at their

19

second meeting, Schmidt, apparently echoing Mellon's letter of invitation to join the committee, "expressed the need for the trustees to consider carefully whether this is the right era in which to start such an expensive project, given the fact that endowment funds of the size needed are so precious." He asked whether "this is the best project that the Foundation can do in our time."[42] Then the committee would have to consider whether the institute should be affiliated with a university or remain independent, as Cairns advocated, and whether it should be established in Washington. It would also have to consider whether the institute should be a private one limited to encouraging scholarship or one with some sort of wider goals as well, including influencing public life, such as Cairns proposed.

Over the next two years the committee met fourteen times, often to discuss the project with an outside consultant. Mellon attended several of the meetings, which were often very lively. Discussion ranged broadly over the whole field of American higher education and the role of the humanities in American life. The consultants, who had usually been furnished with Cairns's last memorandum, were informed that the foundation contemplated spending $15 million—not quite the $25 or $30 million Mellon had mentioned in 1953, but still a considerable sum—and were asked for their advice on the best way to use it.

The first to appear before the committee was Cairns himself, making his case for an independent institute in Washington.[43] After giving him a hearing, however, the committee turned next to university administrators. This was a significant decision, for it put Cairns's ideas at some disadvantage. Cairns, as we have seen, distrusted universities and wished the Residence to be independent of them. Many university leaders (including most of those whom the committee for the

Stoddard M. Stevens in 1969

humanities was to consult) were themselves humanists, but Cairns thought that they were too busy and had too many demands to satisfy to give the humanities a proper emphasis. "College Presidents and Deans," he said later, "are hard pressed men facing enormous difficulties, but the Humanities as such are not their business." Since the humanities were not their sole concern, Cairns thought they were not qualified to comment on the Residence.[44] He was probably well aware that they would find much in his plans to which to object.

Apparently it was Stevens who moved the committee to solicit the views of university leaders. Stevens was a very practical man, and he did not have much sympathy for what he regarded as Cairns's impractical ideas. He did not feel Cairns's anxieties about the future of civilization, and did not share his ambitions to create a mission to save it. His conception of what Old Dominion Foundation should be doing was much narrower; he once asked, for instance, whether the Residence would be "a feasible, practicable and wise method of enhancing humanistic scholarship."[45] Enhancing humanistic scholarship was only part, and probably not the most significant part, of what Cairns had in mind. Moreover, Stevens was concerned that the autonomy of the Residence might involve some dangers. At the committee's second meeting he warned that if the trustees went along with Cairns, they would have to do something to ensure that the director of the Residence could not embark on a "mad frolic."[46]

Stevens thought that the Residence would need to be accountable to another organization, but he did not think that Old Dominion Foundation would fit the bill. The trustees were "busy men" and they could not be expected to give continuous attention to the Residence; he did not want something "around their necks."[47] Moreover, since the project was not "in the field of their competence," he did not think the trustees were very well qualified to look after it.[48] Early in the committee's deliberations he wrote to Mellon, "I am and have been rather appalled at the thought of Old Dominion or some subsidiary foundation formed for the purpose working out the plans and choosing a renowned and able director with administrative abilities who would attract first-class fellows to the institute."[49] Stevens thought that the Residence was something to be referred to the experts, and unlike Cairns, he felt instinctively that the experts were to be found in the universities.

In particular, Stevens looked to Harvard. Even before the committee for the humanities was formed, Stevens wrote Beddall, "Personally I would rather have some expression from Harvard, one of the great institutions of learning, deciding this question than to have the board of Old Dominion make the decision even though it had hired half a dozen experts to advise."[50] Because of its prestige as a seat of learning, Harvard was an obvious place for the committee to begin its inquiries. At the same time a number of other circumstances pointed to Harvard: Mrs. Beale's interest in Harvard, its connection with Dumbarton Oaks, and, of course, its economic stake in the establishment of some sort of institute on White-haven Street, about which Stevens showed some solicitude. Harvard was indeed an obvious candidate to be the foundation's assignee under the terms of Mrs. Beale's will, and at the first meeting of the committee for the humanities, the possibility was mentioned of conveying the Whitehaven Street property to Harvard along with funds and entrusting the whole project to the university.[51]

The first of the academic experts the committee consulted, then, was the president of Harvard, Nathan M. Pusey, on November 19, 1958. The committee did not mention to Pusey the idea of giving property and money to Harvard. What

Nathan M. Pusey in the 1950s

is perhaps surprising, given the university's financial interest, was that Pusey did not propose something like it himself. Indeed, despite Harvard's financial interest, Pusey seemed rather unenthusiastic about the whole enterprise. It may be that he did not quite understand all of the implications of Mrs. Beale's will or did not realize that the educational center had to be established on Whitehaven Street in order for Harvard to keep its legacy. In any case, he expressed general disapproval of independent scholarly institutes, arguing that intellectual activities were better suited to a university, or at least to an institute under university supervision. For one thing, he feared that "a small group of young Fellows left to their own devices outside of a university would go to seed." When the committee mentioned the possibility of spending

$15 million, Pusey said he would not advise the foundation to spend so much on such an undertaking. As a university president, he said, he could think of other uses for so much money.[52]

Pusey's objections to the Residence were seconded strongly by others. Grayson Kirk, president of Columbia University, expressed his reservations to Stevens even before the committee began to interview. Kirk applauded the foundation's efforts to encourage the humanities, but he did not think that an independent scholarly institute was the best way to do so. He also confirmed, unwittingly, Cairns's contention that the humanities were neglected in the universities: "As a university administrator, I must admit regretfully that the unsatisfactory state of the humanities is partially due to the humanists' lack of bargaining power in the academic market-place." Like Pusey, he did not think that an institute should be detached from a university and he did not think that Washington, which he did not regard as a great center of learning, was the right place to establish it. Also like Pusey, he thought such institutes were dangerous to scholars: "Group living in a center removed from the stimulus of university life frequently leads to enervating inaction, and not productive activity." Instead of creating "a new retreat for a selected elite," he thought funds would be put to better use supporting research by university teachers. Kirk also feared that the Residence would compete with the universities for eminent classicists, who he thought were already in short supply.[53]

At the end of December 1958 the committee traveled to Princeton University, where it interviewed Robert Goheen, the university's president, and Professor Whitney J. Oates, head of its classics department. Oates thought that Cairns had made the Residence too confined in its interests. He also

25

thought that such an institute should be affiliated with a university and that the fellows should have opportunities to teach. President Goheen, a classicist himself, echoed Kirk. He thought an institute should be located near a great university—and therefore not in Washington. He believed that scholars should teach and "he worried about a group of men *in vacuo* in a residence." As a university president he also worried about losing faculty. He concluded that the best thing to do with a large sum of money—the figure of $15 million was mentioned—was to endow professorships and finance fellowships, which would help scholars *in* the universities.[54]

While in Princeton the committee also interviewed Professor Harold F. Cherniss of the Institute for Advanced Study, the first member of an independent institute the committee consulted. Cherniss favored independence for the Residence: if it were affiliated with a university, the university would probably "swallow" it "or . . . use it for its own ends, or the ends of its departments." Perhaps surprisingly, however (given his personal situation), Cherniss did not seem notably enthusiastic about the Residence. He proposed that what was needed was not another ivory tower but an institute to train secondary school teachers in the classics, emphasizing that "to aid classics and Humanities the proper place is in secondary schools."[55]

President A. Whitney Griswold of Yale also expressed strong reservations about the Residence when the committee interviewed him in February 1959. By then most of these were familiar. Griswold feared competition for university faculty, and he thought "the humanist should not be placed in an ivory tower." (Curiously, Griswold and others objected that the Residence would be an "ivory tower" when Cairns intended that it should engage with the world at large in order to influence it; either they missed the point or Cairns had not

26

expressed himself very clearly.) "What is needed," Griswold argued, "is to infuse the Humanities into the mainstream of American education." It would be self-defeating to set up an institute that detracted from the universities' ability to promote the humanities; it "would be setting up competition against the few existing forces working to the same end." Griswold concluded that "the proposed Residence was not the best way for the Foundation to aid the Humanities and not a very promising way at best."[56]

In general, then, university opinion of the Residence was quite unfavorable. As Beddall reported in January 1959, even before the committee had finished with its first round of interviews, the committee's consultants did not endorse the idea of an independent institute in Washington and thought there were better ways to help the humanities.[57] They preferred more conventional aid for the humanities within the universities, such as grants to scholars and fellowships for graduate students—"plain, unromantic things," as Jacques Barzun called them later.[58] At best, such support would only encourage the sort of academic scholarship of which Cairns apparently disapproved and would not promote the wider objects he had in mind. But the university presidents did not share Cairns's apocalyptic fears about the future of civilization; they feared mainly the threats the Residence seemed to pose to their own institutions.

THE OBJECTIONS from the universities may not have impressed Cairns, but they seem to have impressed the Old Dominion Foundation trustees, and particularly Stoddard Stevens, who had proposed to meet with the presidents in the first place. While Cairns discounted their opinions, Stevens took them to heart. In April 1959 he remarked at a meeting of the committee that if the university presidents were opposed, "then the project had two strikes against it."[59] Meanwhile, his initial prejudice against independent institutes had been reinforced by further consultation and observation. For some reason, Dumbarton Oaks had made a bad impression on Stevens—he remarked several times that the committee thought it "was not an unqualified success"—and the Institute for Advanced Study an even worse one.[60] Whereas Cairns thought that the latter was the best of the research institutes that had served as models for the Residence, Stevens was not favorably disposed to it after his visit to Princeton. His conversations with Cherniss, he said later, "convinced him that the Foundation does not want to create another Institute for Advanced Study, without discipline and objectives."[61] Stevens's objections to the institute were not very clear, but one thing of which he apparently disapproved was the fact that its members were not required to teach.

Stevens, then, was probably willing to listen when he was approached by a Harvard representative in December 1958. The foundation and the university appeared to have complementary interests. While Old Dominion Foundation could help Harvard secure Mrs. Beale's legacy, Harvard might be of service to the foundation in establishing the Residence or a similar institute. Most important, a university could provide the Residence with the "discipline" Stevens thought it needed but which he did not think the foundation could provide—a fact which was pointed out by a member of the committee for the humanities (who exactly, the minutes do not record) at its second meeting.[62] For this role, Harvard was obviously a strong candidate.

The Harvard Corporation was naturally anxious to secure Mrs. Beale's legacy—more anxious than Pusey had appeared at first—and had evidently delegated one of its members, R. Keith Kane, to approach Stevens. Kane, like Stevens, was

R. Keith Kane in the 1950s

a senior partner in a New York City law firm. Their discussions, then and later, played an important role in the formation of the Center for Hellenic Studies. However, for a long time these discussions seemed to suffer from misunderstanding. Kane appeared to be overly optimistic about what the foundation would be willing to do on Harvard's behalf. While Stevens saw some advantages to Harvard's involvement if the foundation established an institute on Whitehaven Street, and he was willing to help Harvard retain Mrs. Beale's legacy, he was never planning to give the university a blank check. According to Stevens's own report to the other trustees of Old Dominion Foundation, he was noncommittal when he and Kane first talked in December.[63] According to Kane's reports to Harvard, however, Stevens appeared eager to make an arrangement with Harvard. After they met again a few weeks later (at Stevens's initiative), Kane reported that he "came away with the distinct impression that Mr. Stevens would like to do business with Harvard."[64] Kane was struck by two facts in his discussions with Stevens. Stevens and the other trustees of Old Dominion Foundation were not favorably inclined to Washington as a site for the institute—influenced, apparently, by the objections they had heard from university presidents. Second, they had plenty of money to spend—as much as $25 million—and seemed quite ready to spend it.

Harvard did not need to have anything directly to do with the Residence or similar institute on Whitehaven Street in order to secure Mrs. Beale's legacy; all that was required was that an institute be established there by someone. But Kane and others saw in the foundation's apparent eagerness to spend a large sum of money an opportunity for Harvard to benefit by its involvement. The way seemed clear for Harvard to make a proposal to Old Dominion Foundation, and in February 1959 Kane outlined to Stevens in some detail a procedure for the foundation to convey the Whitehaven Street property to Harvard, along with a sum of money, in order to establish an institute for classical studies.[65] Meanwhile, at Harvard, Pusey appointed a faculty committee to prepare a formal proposal, which was submitted to the foundation on February 19.

Harvard seemed to seize eagerly on the idea of an institute devoted in part to publicizing Hellenism or Hellenic values, as Old Dominion Foundation was apparently contemplating. In a letter accompanying the proposal, Pusey remarked that the members of the Harvard committee felt "an excited interest in the plan the Old Dominion Foundation has had in mind, and are in enthusiastic agreement with its underlying assumption that there is pressing need in our currently confused society for the kind of emphasis an institute for the humanities could exert in our common life." The proposal continued this theme. The authors spoke of maintaining "contact with the public domain" and of an "active purpose . . . to communicate to the country in a dignified and persuasive way the nature of the humane ideal of life that originated in ancient Greece." "In this contentious time," they concluded, "the steadying influence of these enduring values that have come from Greece can equip us as a nation to exercise our proper share of leadership in a world become almost rootless."[66]

On the other hand, as well as communicating the humane way of life to the public, the proposed institute would also support scholarly research. These two functions—public communication and scholarly research—would be carried out in two different locations, Washington and Cambridge. Fontaine C. Bradley, an attorney of counsel to Harvard in Washington, had advised that a scholarly center would be needed on Whitehaven Street to fulfill the conditions of Mrs. Beale's will, but in the Harvard plan, scholarship was reserved for Cambridge.[67] Kane told Stevens that he thought the courts would interpret the will liberally since Harvard could show a difficulty in attracting scholars to Washington.[68]

The trouble with this proposal was that its chief purpose was evidently to benefit Harvard, and not necessarily to help Old Dominion Foundation in its efforts to advance the humanities generally. The authors apparently wrote what they thought the Old Dominion Foundation trustees wanted to hear, but the professions of interest in Hellenistic propaganda were vague—as vague as Cairns had been—and sounded insincere. The proposal's "lofty" language[69] did not disguise the fact that Harvard's true interest in an institute in Washington was rather limited and that its main ambition was to acquire a substantial sum of money to spend in Cambridge, though it would be used to support humanistic research. Siegfried Kracauer, a critic of the cinema who often advised the foundation on projects it was considering, observed, "the whole proposition is evidently an expedient calculated to conform to the terms of the will and yet make the Harvard campus its main beneficiary."[70] Jacques Barzun advised the trustees that the proposal was nothing more than "florid, highbrow advertising" for Harvard.[71]

Mellon was not impressed, expressing a disinclination to "turning over the land to Harvard for a token institute."[72] Kane had apparently failed to understand Stevens fully. He may have exaggerated Stevens's dislike of Washington; according to Stevens, it was Harvard officials who emphasized Washington's unsuitability.[73] Attributing such views to him may have been wishful thinking on Kane's part. Kane seemed to think that Stevens and the other Old Dominion trustees were prepared to agree to whatever Harvard suggested, but it would have to do much better than this first proposal to arouse the foundation's interest.

THE COMMITTEE for the humanities paid little attention to the Harvard proposal; it was not diverted immediately from its task. When the committee met in April 1959, Mellon, who attended the meeting, announced that "all of the issues still are to be decided."[74] Now, having learned the views of university presidents, the committee wished to consider another point of view, by canvassing non-academic intellectual opinion, beginning with the eminent journalist Walter Lippmann. Lippmann, however, did not seem much more sympathetic to the Residence than the university presidents had been, sharing many of their assumptions and prejudices. (One observer, apparently a supporter of the Residence, commented, "Lippmann is pro-university maybe because he is not himself an academic. He has an idealistic view of university atmosphere.")[75] Lippmann thought the Residence should be located near a great university, if not necessarily formally affiliated with it. Washington, he thought, was unsuitable because it did not have such a university. Also, "because Washington is an operating center, he did not think its cultural climate is favorable to thinking." Washingtonians were "not worrying about clarifying the basic issues of western culture." Cairns's aim, apparently, was to change that.

In October 1959 the committee interviewed Mortimer Adler, director of the Institute for Philosophic Research. Adler argued that the Residence could make a contribution only if the fellows engaged in a "disciplined common work," such as his own institute promoted. He did not approve of research centers like the Institute for Advanced Study, whose fellows were not obliged to collaborate. Unfortunately, he observed, senior scholars were not likely to agree to engage in common work, and junior fellows appeared to be the only hope for a cooperative enterprise. (This discussion, incidentally, pointed up again the vagueness and ambiguity of Cairns's plan; there was some disagreement among the committee members about whether or not Cairns did in fact intend the fellows of the Residence to collaborate.) If a cooperative enterprise could not be established, Adler recommended that the foundation support existing institutions such as St. John's College or finance fellowships in the humanities.[76]

The most severe criticism of Cairns's Residence was offered by another academic scholar and administrator, Jacques Barzun, dean of the faculties and provost at Columbia University. The committee evidently took his views very seriously and gave him several opportunities to express them, interviewing him twice, in June and September 1959, and also inviting him to comment in writing. Barzun's critique was extremely damning. He thought the whole proposal suffered from a "radical ambiguity." It was not clear whether the fellows were supposed to be trying to save civilization or behave as scholars. He asked, "Are the resident fellows to shelter and comfort one another against the barbarian tide, so that a later day may be brightened by their example; or are they simply scholars who will do research and publish results in the ordinary way?" He feared that although the Residence was supposed to have a larger purpose, because of the way it was constituted, it would never fulfill this goal. Cairns, he said, "thinks a small group of fellows in the Residence would act as he wants them to, while all experience points the other way." The Residence would turn into another scholarly retreat, much like those that existed already. Because of the "general obsession with research," the Residence would not exercise any important influence on national culture. When all was said and done, the Residence would merely add to the "already swollen stream" of academic scholarship. "None of this," he concluded, "sounds like the influence, leadership, and 'vital humanism' proposed as the main object of the Residence."

Barzun argued that the best way to help the humanities was "to do a few plain, unromantic things, rather than something new and spectacular," pointing particularly to the need to remedy the reliance of universities on untrained graduate students to teach undergraduates. The Residence would take teachers away from the universities, at a time when good teachers were badly needed where they were. Barzun thought there had to be a better balance between scholarship and teaching. The Residence would not contribute to this but upset the balance even further: "an institute would not encourage teaching but only an obsession with books and learned papers, of which we have too many already."[77]

To OPPOSE this varied criticism of the Residence, Cairns managed to find only a little support. He solicited the favorable testimony of the director of Dumbarton Oaks, John S. Thacher, and the director of the Folger Shakespeare Library (also in Washington), Louis B. Wright, and also obtained what seemed to be a rather vague endorsement by Marshall Clagett, head of the humanities center in Wisconsin and a scholar of ancient and medieval science, who wrote that the Residence would "give a very much needed boost to the Humanities, which have become the stepchild of modern education."[78] However, of those the committee for the humanities consulted directly, only Jackson Mathews endorsed the Residence enthusiastically. Mathews was vice-president of Bollingen Foundation and general editor of the foundation's English edition of the works of Paul Valéry. In February 1959 Mathews submitted a memorandum to the foundation in which he endorsed Cairns's ideas and criticized the universities for their objections. The universities, he said, "are confused about the nature and importance of the humanities and indeed about their own motives with regard to the Residence."[79] (By now, however, Cairns himself seemed to be retreating from the anti-university theme, even appearing to argue that Washington was a suitable site since it was "a university town.")[80] When the committee for the humanities spoke with him in May, Mathews said that the Residence was "much the best" of all the proposals the foundation had received, and he expressed "astonishment" that its merits had not been recognized generally.[81]

This was not a great deal, however; the tide was clearly running against the Residence. In November 1959 Cairns wrote another memorandum to answer his critics. He began with a quotation from the classicist Gilbert Murray (perhaps best known for his translations of Greek tragedies) warning, "The next generation must use all its strength, all its wisdom, to see that the main drift of the world is Hellenic and not barbarous." However, in general Cairns's new memorandum seemed less inspired by apocalyptic fears than some of his earlier ones. He protested that the committee for the humanities had interviewed the wrong people. Instead of "the men who have made the Humanities the business of their lives," the committee had consulted university administrators, who had too many other concerns to have time to attend to the humanities properly. "I will affirm," he concluded, "that the idea of the Residence stands in need of a most careful appraisal at the hands of men who know the present almost desperate plight of the Humanities." Again, however, Cairns appeared now to be downplaying the anti-university aspect of the Residence and even suggested that the Residence would actually serve the universities.[82]

On December 9, 1959, Cairns appeared before the committee once more to make his case, proposing that the foundation engage someone to interview "real humanists." Stevens, however, appeared unsympathetic. He summarized the case against the Residence, reporting the virtually unanimous opposition of the committee's consultants. He was convinced that the foundation should not create another independent institute, without a clear purpose and without "discipline." He noted further that the foundation was under increasing pressure to achieve something and that the trustees wanted "to produce a respectable result."[83]

Faced with these objections, Cairns submitted a new proposal for something he called the "Palladium," a modest establishment to sponsor lectures, seminars, and publications.

The advantages he proposed were that it could be set up relatively quickly on Whitehaven Street in order to save Mrs. Beale's bequest for Harvard and—more important from his own point of view—that it could be used to test, relatively inexpensively, the concept of the Residence. "If the idea proves to be a sound one," Cairns wrote, "the Residence will grow naturally from this beginning."[84] The foundation submitted the proposal to Mathews and Kracauer for their opinions. Mathews agreed with Cairns, but Kracauer said that the Palladium would not be a true test for the Residence since it would be erected on different principles. The Palladium appeared to be an ordinary scholarly institute and would not evolve naturally into anything like the Residence. The experiment, then, would prove nothing.[85]

The submission of the new proposal to Kracauer and Mathews appears to have been somewhat perfunctory. By now it was fairly obvious that the foundation would not proceed with the Residence as Cairns conceived it. At the end of January 1960 the committee for the humanities decided not to proceed with the Palladium, and to inform Cairns of "the tentative negative conclusions of the Committee" regarding the Residence.[86] Cairns's wife made one last attempt to save it, writing to the committee in February 1960. She blamed the university presidents, who, "faced with the idea of the proposed Residence, want the money for their own institutions; also they do not relish our criticism of themselves, and their schools." But this did not find much favor with the foundation's advisers.[87] Old Dominion Foundation's interest in Cairns's proposal was effectively at an end.

I T WAS NOW a very good question whether the foundation would decide to do anything at all on Whitehaven Street. The advice of all the committee's consultants had been

almost completely discouraging. The whole scheme underlying the Residence or similar institute had proved so full of
difficulties that it seemed impossible to salvage much of anything from the committee's deliberations. It appeared increasingly likely that the foundation would start over again and
look for completely new and different ways to help advance
the humanities.

Meanwhile, Harvard, which remained deeply interested in
Old Dominion Foundation's decision, had submitted a second proposal. This new proposal came about as the result of
a meeting between Stevens and Kane in the middle of 1959.
Stevens, as we have seen, had not been terribly impressed by
Harvard's initial proposal, but he continued to express some
concern about the university's position with respect to Mrs.
Beale's legacy. Already by July 1959 Stevens, seeing the way
the committee's opinion on the Residence was tending,
wanted to give Harvard fair warning. He met with Kane,
therefore, and told him, as he related later to the other Old
Dominion trustees, that "there was a possibility which had
not ripened into a probability" that the committee would recommend against the establishment of an institute on Whitehaven Street.[88] In that case, presumably, the foundation
would convey the property to Harvard so that Harvard could
have a chance to save the legacy.

Stevens apparently wished to alert Harvard so that it could
make plans to establish, on its own, an institute that would
satisfy the courts, without the participation, financial or otherwise, of Old Dominion Foundation.[89] Kane, however,
seems to have missed the point. While Stevens thought he
was warning Harvard to prepare for the worst, Kane thought
that Stevens was inviting Harvard to submit a new proposal.[90] Stevens was apparently willing to hear such a pro-

posal, but according to his own account, he did not solicit it; rather Kane *offered* it.[91] Kane remained optimistic, assuming that Old Dominion Foundation wanted to deal with Harvard and that the trustees were still thinking of spending as much as $25 million on a university-affiliated institute.

Pusey had delegated the writing of the initial Harvard proposal to a committee of faculty members, but he composed the second himself. After showing it around the university for comments, he submitted it to Old Dominion Foundation in September 1959. In its broad outlines, the proposal resembled the earlier one: an institute for classical studies divided geographically between Cambridge and Washington, with the two parts performing different functions. Cambridge would be the scholarly center and Washington "the administrative center . . . and a place of meeting for the project with its wider publics." There the center would try to influence national life, "to strengthen the role of Hellenism in contemporary culture." Pusey apparently assumed still that the foundation endorsed the broader goals Cairns had suggested, and he retained some of Cairns's aims and language. He wrote that if the foundation conveyed money and property to Harvard,

It is my understanding that the responsibility incurred with the conveyance would be a double one: first, to establish and operate a Center to encourage scholarship in Hellenism, and second, to seek to extend the influence of Hellenism in our society. The effort is motivated by the conviction that the achievement of the classical Greeks has been of special importance in Western Civilization and that it is desirable now to strengthen its influence in the contemporary world.

Pusey added little to what had been said about the Washington center in the first Harvard proposal. He did, how-

39

ever, say a great deal more about the scholarly center in Cambridge, a subject to which he had obviously given some thought. The first proposal had been vague even about the Cambridge half of the institute; now Pusey had a more definite plan. Weighing the various needs of the profession, Pusey decided that the center would do well to give particular encouragement to younger scholars, who were often "isolated in small departments in indifferent communities," struggling "to get on with writing in hours saved from teaching." For these young men and women, an extended period of freedom and leisure spent in a classical institute in Cambridge could be extremely beneficial.[92]

Certain features of Pusey's institute were modeled on another scholarly organization at Harvard, the Society of Fellows, which had been founded in 1932. (Indeed, Pusey spoke of his new institute as a "society.") The Society of Fellows had both junior fellows, who were given as long as six years to pursue independent study, and senior fellows, who were members of the Harvard faculty and administration. All of the fellows, junior and senior, dined together once a week, with the object of encouraging intellectual exchange among different disciplines and generations.[93] Similarly, the Cambridge classical institute that Pusey proposed would also have senior fellows, who, along with the junior fellows, "should come together at regular intervals to enjoy the benefits of common social life."

This institute or society would be costly. Pusey proposed an annual budget of about $728,500, which was larger than that of Dumbarton Oaks. If the budget were to be provided out of endowment income, the endowment would have to be about $15 million. In addition, $2 million would be needed for a building or buildings in Washington and perhaps another $1 million for a building in Cambridge.

Pusey's proposal represented a considerable advance over the proposal made in February; it evidently had a well considered purpose. Unfortunately for Harvard, it seemed still to be based on rather optimistic views of what Old Dominion Foundation would be willing to do on its behalf. Although Pusey had taken into consideration other aims besides the advantage of Harvard, benefiting Harvard still seemed its chief purpose, and any interests Old Dominion Foundation had on Whitehaven Street quite secondary. The university was still the main beneficiary—for which the foundation would be put to considerable expense. Kane had thought that the foundation would be willing to contribute generously to Harvard in Cambridge if Harvard would administer a small public institute in Washington. But this assumption was apparently rooted in misunderstanding. The Old Dominion trustees were not very impressed with the proposal—in fact, they seem hardly to have discussed it—and in December 1959 (about the same time the committee for the humanities was also putting an end to the Residence), Stevens met with Kane to deliver the bad news. Kane reported that Stevens and his fellow trustees feared that the Harvard proposal "might be a subterfuge to qualify under the Beale will and be a waste of money." Moreover, Stevens said the sums Pusey proposed would undermine the foundation's finances.[94] Pusey's figures were not inconsistent with the sum—$15 million—that had been mentioned in connection with the Residence, but by now such numbers seemed out of proportion. The trustees' interest in grandiose schemes had declined, and along with it, apparently, their willingness to spend so much money.

S TEVENS'S REMARKS came as a great shock to Kane. His optimism evaporated, and on the last day of 1959 he wrote in alarm to Pusey that "Harvard's legacy from Mrs. Beale is in serious jeopardy."[95] Harvard now faced a difficult prospect. Apparently Old Dominion Foundation would soon assign the Whitehaven Street property to Harvard, without financial assistance, leaving the university to devise some means to save the Beale legacy on its own. What made the situation worse, it began to appear to Harvard officials that an inexpensive, "token" institute such as had been proposed earlier would not be sufficient; Harvard would have to establish (on its own) "something substantial."[96] However, as Kane pointed out, something substantial might make "no economic sense."[97] There would be little point in creating an institute to save Mrs. Beale's legacy if the institute were to cost a large part of what the legacy was worth.

But Harvard proved fortunate after all. Gradually, over the next few months, university and foundation officials found common ground. Stevens proved still willing to consider a Harvard proposal to advance the humanities—provided that it was a scheme that interested the foundation, that seemed to promise help for the humanities, that was not enormously expensive, and that was not, in Kracauer's words, merely "an expedient calculated to conform to the terms of the will and yet make the Harvard campus its main beneficiary." Harvard finally made such a proposal.

Kane and Stevens remained in contact after Stevens delivered his discouraging news in December. Stevens in fact indicated in January 1960 that Old Dominion Foundation might be willing to give Harvard a grant for a project to aid the humanities, a project which he stipulated "should be kept quite separate from the Washington problem and Mrs. Beale's legacy and devise."[98] Stevens perhaps wished to soften the blow he had given Harvard in December. Instead of a proposal to advance the humanities unrelated to the Washington problem, however, Pusey tried once more with a proposal for Whitehaven Street. This time, at last, his idea proved a spark that ignited Stevens's and Mellon's interest.

Pusey's proposal was closely related to the one he had presented in September 1959. It involved an institute whose main purpose was to benefit young classicists. The main departure from the earlier proposal was that the institute would now be located in Washington, on Whitehaven Street, rather than in Cambridge. At the same time, Pusey wished to preserve his original idea of "a community of scholars somewhat similar to the Society of Fellows at Harvard, or even to a Medieval University," although this would be harder to create in Washington than in Cambridge. In Cambridge, the Harvard classics department would have provided the senior fellows. Now, since Pusey did not think that senior scholars should be taken permanently from their university posts to reside at the center, the senior fellows would only visit from Harvard and other universities; they would not be a more or less continuous presence, as they would have been in Cambridge. Nonetheless, Pusey expected the senior fellows to visit frequently, to attend "almost weekly meetings or dinners," and he hoped that an inter-generational intellectual society could still be created despite the altered circumstances.[99]

Pusey's proposal in large part answered the various objections that had been made to the earlier Harvard proposals. It was not merely a subterfuge to benefit Harvard, and it appeared that it could be established at a fairly reasonable ex-

43

pense. Most important, it held real interest for the foundation as a way to contribute to the advancement of the humanities. When Pusey and Kane met with Stevens to outline his idea in April, Stevens said that it interested him and that it might well interest Mellon.[100] The next month Pusey was given the opportunity to present his ideas to Mellon directly. They met to discuss the proposed institute on May 20, 1960, when Pusey suggested that it could be operated with a budget of about $150,000 per annum.

Now, however, it was Pusey's turn to be cautious. Whereas in the past he had suggested that the foundation convey both property and money to the university, now he was careful about involving Harvard too directly with the institute. Harvard, he said, "would step out once the center was organized." Stevens, still concerned about ensuring that any center the foundation established would be subject to some form of "discipline," said that "he assumed Harvard would maintain a moral obligation to step in if the institute went downhill, as perhaps would other universities who furnished senior fellows."[101] Pusey was evidently being careful at this point not to identify Harvard too closely with the proposed institute so as not to commit the university to the burdens of administering it without financial assistance. And, having been proved wrong in their optimism, Harvard officials tended to be pessimistic about what Old Dominion Foundation would be willing to do. Kane for one now thought that the foundation would not give the university all or even most of what was needed.[102]

Kane thought the meeting was "inconclusive," but Pusey's proposal was beginning to arouse some interest. Hoping to move matters along, Pusey set out in his car in the summer of 1960 to interview prominent classical scholars on the east coast.[103] He had two objectives: to canvass scholarly opinion on the center and to seek suitable candidates for a director and senior fellows. He reported on his travels at another meeting with the Old Dominion trustees in October, a meeting Kane, Barrett, and Mellon also attended. Pusey said that he had found great interest in an institute of junior fellows among the scholars he had interviewed. He had also succeeded in his search for a director and senior fellows. For fellows, he said he had five men in mind. For director, his first choice was Professor Whitney Oates of Princeton, whom the committee had consulted at the beginning of its deliberations; his next choice was Professor Bernard Knox of Yale.

Pusey now proposed that the institute should be called the Center for Hellenic Studies. Its capital requirements he estimated at about $5 million, including $1 million for building and $4 million for endowment. This sum was substantial enough to make him hesitate still to make a firm offer of Harvard's services. He said it would be a good idea for a university to administer the center, and he thought Harvard was a good choice because of its strength in the classics and his own personal enthusiasm; but, he said, Harvard "was not looking for new enterprises if the Foundation preferred to go to another." Stevens, however, had become convinced by then that Harvard should be given responsibility for the center. He explained that although the foundation would assist in its formation, the trustees, "because of their commitments in other fields, could not take part in permanent leadership." In effect, there was to be a trade. Old Dominion Foundation would provide the funds if Harvard would provide responsible administration. The meeting ended optimistically: "Mr. Mellon . . . expressed approval of a working arrangement with Harvard."[104]

According to Kane, who probably learned it from Stevens, the trustees of Old Dominion Foundation were impressed greatly by Pusey's presentation. Soon after the meeting, the trustees resolved that if Harvard would accept the assignment of Mrs. Beale's property, the foundation would "put up $5 million."[105] On December 7, 1960, the offer was given formal effect. Pusey and Kane met in New York with the Old Dominion trustees. After they withdrew, the trustees resolved unanimously to give Harvard the Whitehaven Street property and the sum of $5 million.[106]

THE ANNOUNCEMENT in January 1961 of the center's establishment met with an enthusiastic response. *The Washington Post* emphasized that it would add significantly to the scholarly and cultural resources of the capital.[107] Emily Vermeule, then of Boston University and later professor of classics at Harvard, wrote to Peter Elder, dean of the Graduate School of Arts and Sciences at Harvard, with congratulations on "the spurt of blood to the head of Hellenic Studies—a marvellous enterprise in spite of being in Washington."[108] Sarah Gibson Blanding, president of Vassar College (recipient of many Mellon benefactions), wrote to Pusey, "It is reassuring to know that in this mad and hurried world, classical studies are not to be neglected and that men of foresight are turning to them for enlightenment to help solve the crucial problems of the future." She added that "Paul Mellon is a true friend of higher education" and that the gift bespoke "the breadth and depth of his understanding of values inherent in the liberal tradition."[109]

Meanwhile there were a great many practical details to attend to. On January 24, 1961, Old Dominion Foundation obtained a court order allowing it to convey its Whitehaven Street property to Harvard University, for such uses as Mrs. Beale had specified in her will. More accurately, the property was to be conveyed to a special Washington, D.C., corpora-

46

tion known as the Trustees for Harvard University, which already owned and administered Dumbarton Oaks. The conveyance was accomplished by a deed dated February 23, 1961.[110] A little later Harvard officials determined that the adjoining property which Old Dominion Foundation had purchased from Harvard in 1956 for the use of the Residence would not be needed for the Center for Hellenic Studies; eventually the foundation sold it to the Italian government for an embassy, which remains unbuilt.[111]

The search for a director was also begun. Pusey himself wanted to serve as acting director until a permanent one was found, and he did so briefly, until the burdens of the Harvard presidency forced him to relinquish the post to Peter Elder. Meanwhile, Pusey's first choice for the permanent position, Whitney J. Oates, had been approached in October 1960, even before the center's formal establishment. Stevens thought Oates should be allowed to "write his own ticket." In November, however, Oates declined because of his commitments at Princeton.[112] Happily, he endorsed Bernard Knox, whom Pusey had already proposed as his next choice and who had impressed Mellon as well.[113] In March 1961 Knox, whose scholarly specialty was Greek tragedy, agreed to become director. When his acceptance was announced, he told the *Yale Daily News* that "the study of Greek is at a critical stage" and that the center could do a great deal "to put Greek back on the map."[114] Knox, however, had arranged to take a sabbatical in 1961–1962 (which he intended to spend in Greece), and he was engaged further as Sather Lecturer at the University of California, Berkeley, for the spring of 1963. Michael Putnam of Brown University, who had been assisting Elder, was thus appointed acting resident director for the first year.

As finally arranged, the center was to have two overseeing

Bernard M.W. Knox in 1978

boards, one consisting of senior fellows and the other, known as the administrative committee, consisting of laymen, who were to be drawn from Harvard and Old Dominion Foundation. In December 1960 both boards were formally appointed by the Trustees for Harvard University.[115] The senior fellows were Knox, Oates, John Finley of Harvard, Richmond Lattimore of Bryn Mawr, and James H. Oliver of Johns Hopkins. After he was appointed director, Knox was replaced by Gerald Else of the University of Michigan. On the administrative committee, Mellon, Schmidt, Stevens, Brooks, Cairns, and David Bruce, the American ambassador to the United Kingdom, formerly married to Mellon's sister, represented Old Dominion Foundation; and Pusey, Kane, and Elder represented Harvard.

It was agreed generally that the center should begin operating immediately, even before it had its own permanent buildings. Luckily, Mellon could offer the center the use of the Tompkins House on Whitehaven Street, which he had purchased in 1957 for possible use by the Residence. In December 1960 the administrative committee and senior fellows, meeting together, toured the house and agreed that it would be a suitable site for the center's first year of operation. Appropriate renovations were carried out in the summer of 1961.[116]

Meanwhile, in January 1961 Elder had dispatched several hundred letters soliciting applications for the inaugural group of junior scholars.[117] He admitted in the letter that all the center could offer at that point was the excitement of an untried venture. There was no library, and he did not know where fellows would live. Still, he received a number of applications, including some from abroad, and the center's first fellows were chosen in April.[118] The fellows assembled in Washington in September and October 1961. They had to find their own living accommodations in Washington, but they had studies and were given lunch at the Tompkins House.

Construction of the permanent buildings began about the time the center opened for its first year in temporary quarters. Page Cross, an architect based in New York City who had designed several buildings for Mellon, was engaged to design the center. Cross had preliminary plans ready by April 1961.[119] As revised in May, his plan provided for a central building with a library, seminar rooms, offices, and studies, as well as a dining room and kitchen. The director would have a separate dwelling, and there would be housing for eight fellows in all—"a unit of 5 family houses built row-style" and a separate building with single rooms.[120] Unfortunately, it was apparent that all of this would cost consider-

49

ably more than the $1 million of the Old Dominion Foundation grant that had been designated for construction. It looked for a time as if the center might have to provide the junior fellows with rental allowances instead of housing. However, that would mean a large drain on the annual budget. Moreover, if the fellows did not live together at the center, it would be difficult to create the intellectual community Pusey and others had in mind.

There was little choice but to accept a higher figure for construction costs, especially since time was pressing and everyone wanted the buildings finished, or largely finished, in time for the center's second year. Harvard and Old Dominion Foundation agreed to share equally the extra costs of construction up to $500,000, but with a firm resolution that this sum should not be exceeded.[121] In July 1961 Cross's revised plans were approved.[122] In August 1961 another hurdle was cleared when the Washington, D.C., Board of Zoning Adjustments awarded an exemption for the center. (The area was zoned for residences and embassies.) In September the George A. Fuller Company was authorized to begin construction.[123]

The plans for the center continued to undergo revision. At one point the planners had decided to have separate dwellings for married fellows after all. Just before construction began, Cross also revised the design for the director's house.[124] In February 1962 he made one more major change to the plan when he altered the design of the main building, moving the kitchen and dining room to the basement and the fellows' studies from a second floor to the main floor of the building, thereby eliminating the need for a second story.[125] These changes and unanticipated costs, which necessitated further alterations, slowed construction.[126] The buildings were not ready as early as had been hoped: although the fellows' houses

Fellows' houses under construction, May 1962.
The view is looking east.

were finished for the second year, the director's residence and
the main building were not. The Tompkins House continued
in use. At last, however, in December 1962, Knox could report that the main building should be finished in March and
the director's house shortly afterwards.[127] The final cost
turned out to be $1,435,131.13—actually a little under bud-
get.[128]

  With all its buildings completed, and all painted white, the
Center for Hellenic Studies assumed the general appearance
and ambience of a village. J. Carter Brown, director of the
National Gallery of Art, has even noted a similarity to Jefferson's "academical village" at the University of Virginia.[129]
Six cottages—the five family houses and the superintendent's
dwelling—are arranged, four on one side and two on the

other, along a drive leading to the front of the administration building, as the main building came to be called. To the left, approaching the administration building, is a long, single-story structure with accommodation for three single fellows as well as for guests; it became known informally as the "bachelors' quarters." Behind the administration building is the director's residence.

Appropriately, the architectural focus of the center is the building that houses the library. Fortunately, the center had a library to put in it. The difficulties of creating a usable classics library from nothing had been one of the greatest worries during the center's planning. (That had been one of Pusey's arguments for locating a classical institute at Harvard, where it would have had the use of one of the world's great libraries.) The center opened in the Tompkins House with only a handful of books, although Putnam began ordering more as rapidly as he could.[130] Knox wrote later that "the Fellows of that year still remember the excitement with which they greeted every fresh parcel of books, each one hoping it would contain the volume he needed."[131] (Actually, one fellow pointed out that there was an advantage in having few books to read; there was less excuse to put off writing.)[132] Putnam hoped that the center might acquire a good private library, and he sent to Blackwell's in Oxford asking if they knew of any for sale. He wrote, "What we really most need is a first-rate nucleus of the basic texts, commentaries and reference works. I don't envision another Bodleian or a Widener. Still, we want a good working library, cutting as broad a swathe through the various disciplines as possible."[133]

Soon afterwards, the center obtained a private library as extensive as Putnam could have wished, although the manner was unfortunate. In the autumn of 1961 Werner Jaeger, a very eminent classical scholar who was a member of the Harvard

52

The administration building before it was painted white.
The photograph was taken shortly after the center
was dedicated.

faculty, died suddenly. Jaeger had shown an interest in the
center before his death and was even planning to visit it. His
widow was willing to have the center acquire his large library, which she wished to keep intact. John Finley, who had
been Jaeger's colleague at Harvard and was one of the center's
senior fellows, worked loyally on the center's behalf. In January 1962 the administrative committee authorized the pur-
chase of the library, which was then catalogued at Harvard.[134]
By the end of 1962 the books were available to the fellows in
Washington. Jaeger's library was soon joined by large por-
tions of the private libraries of Arthur Stanley Pease and Arthur Darby Nock, two other Harvard classics professors who
died in the center's early years, leaving their books to Harvard. Thus given a good start, the library grew rapidly by
means of a generous budget for acquisitions. In 1971 Knox

Dedication of the Center for Hellenic Studies, May 14, 1963

Left: Nathan Pusey speaking. Bernard Knox is seated
at left and Paul Mellon at right.
Right: Paul Mellon speaking. Nathan Pusey is seated behind him.

Above: Archibald MacLeish
and Paul Mellon
At left: Bernard Knox speaking

Guests touring the center, with the fellows' houses
in the background

Guests touring the center, with the
director's residence in the background

wrote, "at the threshold of its tenth year of existence the Center can take pride in the building of a library which in spite of its late beginning is adequate in most of the many branches of the discipline it represents and more than adequate in some."[135] By 1986 the center's holdings numbered about 43,000 volumes.

Arrangements were also being made for publication of the fellows' own books. Publication had always been an important objective of the center's planners, and a great deal of thought was given to it. The budget contained generous sums for publishing. Knox opened negotiations with the Harvard University Press when he returned from Greece, and they settled on a monograph series. However, he and press officials disagreed on the matter of final approval of manuscripts. Knox thought that the *imprimatur* of the center's director and senior fellows should be sufficient, but the press wanted to submit manuscripts to an outside reader as well. In the end, it was decided that the center should be its own publisher, with the Harvard press acting as manufacturer and distributor.

By the spring of 1963, then, the center had been set on its feet. Two groups of fellows—thirteen in all—had spent a year at the center and proved its value. A library was in place, and arrangements in hand for publishing the fellows' own books. And finally, in the spring of 1963, the center had completed buildings, ready to be dedicated. The dedication ceremony was assured of a large and distinguished audience because of an interesting coincidence. It happened that President Kennedy was a member of the Harvard Board of Overseers, the larger of the university's two governing bodies, and was approaching the end of his term. In Kennedy's honor, both the Board of Overseers and Harvard's other governing body, the corporation (known formally as the President and Fellows of

Harvard College) decided to meet in Washington in May, only the second time since the founding of Harvard in the seventeenth century that they had met outside of Cambridge. Their meeting would include visits to Harvard's Washington outposts. They would tour Dumbarton Oaks on May 13 and dine at the White House in the evening. The next day, May 14, 1963, was appointed for the dedication of the permanent buildings of the Center for Hellenic Studies. President Kennedy was unable to attend, but it was an impressive occasion nonetheless. Mellon, Knox, and the poet Archibald Mac-Leish, Boylston Professor of Rhetoric and Oratory at Harvard, all delivered addresses, later published together in a small book. Mellon outlined the history of the idea of the center and expressed his hope that it might serve as a model for other institutions. Knox expressed his hopes that the center would "give not only a fresh impetus but also a new direction to the study of Greek and hence to its effect on our own age." Among other things, MacLeish complimented Mellon for his generosity, commenting that the center was a "gift which, like all his gifts, is as remarkable for its grace and its imagination as for its munificence."[136]

THE CENTER'S HISTORY since May 1963 is told relatively quickly. Once it was established in its own buildings, it changed very little—with the significant exception of its budget, which, because of the effects of inflation, rose from about $216,000 per annum in 1962–1963 to about $700,000 in 1986–1987. Fortunately, the center has been able to count on Paul Mellon's continuing interest; he was still an active member of the center's administrative committee as of 1990. Stevens also long continued to take a keen interest in the center, serving on the administrative committee until his death in 1981. Mellon and Stevens were both trustees of the

John Finley with junior fellow Masaaki Kubo (1962–1963)
and family

Andrew W. Mellon Foundation, formed by a merger of Old
Dominion and Avalon foundations, which made substantial
contributions to increase the center's endowment in 1969 and
1977. More recently, the foundation gave the center $245,000
to catalogue its library.

Bernard Knox (left) and visitor in front of the
"bachelors' quarters"

The work of the center otherwise goes on quietly. Already
in 1966 Knox, using a phrase from Aristotle, said that the
center had "attained its natural form," from which it has not
varied much in succeeding years.[137] The board of senior fellows chooses eight junior fellows every year. (This is the se-

nior fellows' main function; because of the impracticality of frequent visits by scholars with posts in universities distant from Washington, Pusey's hope of a Washington Society of Fellows was never realized.) They try to achieve a rough equality of representatives of the basic humanistic disciplines of history, literature, and philosophy. Intellectual diversity is matched by cultural diversity, as the center has always drawn fellows from abroad as well as from American universities. Although Americans predominate, a third or more of the junior fellows have come from foreign countries—and not only the western European nations well known for their classical scholarship. In 1989–1990 the center had its first fellow (and indeed, its first candidate) from the Soviet Union. (A complete list of fellows, along with their topics, is provided in the appendix.)

Although intellectual exchange is naturally encouraged, few demands are made upon the fellows' time once they are in residence. They eat lunch together, along with the director, five days a week, a setting that often produces quite lively discussion. They hear talks by visitors, who come once or twice a month. "Our usual procedure," Knox explained to a prospective speaker in 1962, "is for the visitor to have lunch with the Fellows and afterwards, over coffee, address them. The discussion usually goes on until late in the afternoon."[138] Over time, these presentations have become somewhat more formal. Also, since 1964–1965 the fellows have made formal presentations of their own work, usually after Christmas. But aside from these activities, the fellows are free to do as they please. The fellows are given keys to the library so they can read all night if they wish. The center is organized to give them the greatest possible freedom and leisure to pursue their own studies.

IN SOME WAYS the center's routine (or rather absence of routine) seems contrary to the stated intentions of the center's founders, who apparently intended that it should play a more active and public role. Pusey had proposed that it should be "a center for planning strategy for the advance of Hellenism in this country and abroad," and the press release announcing its establishment stated similar ambitions.[139] But such notions were apparently left over from consideration of the Residence and related proposals and were not meant very earnestly. The center was not structured or situated to exercise broad public influence. Its fellows were young scholars from the universities whose efforts would be directed, inevitably, to the production of scholarly books and articles to help them advance their academic careers. The Center for Hellenic Studies was even less suited to humanistic propaganda than the Residence would have been.

But if the center failed to save the world or to re-infuse it with the values of Hellenism, on its own terms it has nevertheless made a significant contribution to the humanities, both in America and abroad. The classics have suffered a general decline since the time when every educated person knew Latin and many knew Greek. Because of their historic significance in the development of western civilization, it has seemed important to encourage the tradition of classical learning, even if confined to professional classicists. To this mission the center has made a notable contribution, adding appreciably to the scholarly understanding of the culture and society of the ancient Greeks. No doubt many of the fellows would have done their work in any case, but the center, with the opportunities it provides for sustained, uninterrupted study and contemplation, has certainly acted as midwife for a great deal of interesting and significant scholarship.

The administration building as it appears today

In the most tangible terms, the fellows have written, collectively, a small library of books and articles while they were in Washington. A number of the fellows' books have appeared under the center's own imprint. The arrangement with the Harvard press, which resulted in the publication of half a dozen volumes, ended in 1973 when the center found it too expensive to continue acting as its own publisher, but Knox negotiated a more conventional publishing arrangement with the Princeton University Press a few years later.

The fellows themselves have testified eagerly to the benefits they received from their year at the center. In 1979, on the occasion of Knox's sixty-fifth birthday, over fifty former fellows contributed essays to a *Festschrift* in his honor. The book's preface stated:

ever since the Center's beginnings in 1961, an ever growing community of former junior fellows has been spreading all over the world—ex-centrics they might be called—cherishing memories of the year at "The Center" and drawing on the stimulating experience and the progress achieved in this place. Many recent publications can be seen to contain an introductory remark acknowledging the importance of the year at the Center for the growth and final outcome of the work.[140]

More such testimony was produced when Knox retired from the directorship in 1985, after nearly twenty-five years of distinguished service. He was succeeded by Professor Zeph Stewart of Harvard, who had served for many years as a member of the center's administrative committee. Stewart held a reception in Knox's honor at the center in December 1985. Paul Mellon was unable to attend, but Nathan Pusey, by then long retired from the Harvard presidency (and also from the presidency of the Andrew W. Mellon Foundation), was present. Also in attendance was a large number of center alumni, who presented Knox with a volume of letters expressing their appreciation of him and of the Center for Hellenic Studies. They represented a group that numbered almost 190 (almost 230 by 1990), who were teaching the classics in university posts all over the world.

APPENDIX

THE JUNIOR FELLOWS,
WITH THEIR NATIONALITIES AND THEIR TOPICS

1961–1962

John K. Davies (U.K.), A prosopography of Athenian landed families from the sixth to the third century

Anna Morpurgo (Italy), A survey of the Boeotian dialect; a lexicon of Linear B

Douglass S. Parker (U.S.), Translations of early plays of Aristophanes; a critique of *The Acharnians*

Kenneth J. Reckford (U.S.), Euripides

Hans-Peter Stahl (Germany), Thucydides

Garry Wills (U.S.), Aeschylus; the *Antigone* of Sophocles

1962–1963

Jean-Claude Carrière (France), Political ideas of Plutarch

John P.A. Gould (U.K.), Euripides and Lysias; a study of the literature of the late fifth and early fourth centuries

John J. Keaney, Jr. (U.S.), An edition of Harpokration

Masaaki Kubo (Japan), The importance of the mask in Greek tragedy

Walther Ludwig (Germany), Hellenistic epigrams and the relations between New and Roman comedy

Hubert Martin, Jr. (U.S.), Plutarch's biographical theory and method

William Whallon (U.S.), Homer; Aeschylus

1963–1964

Harry C. Avery (U.S.), A prosopographical study of the Four Hundred

Henry Steele Commager, Jr. (U.S.), The remains of Hellenistic literature and its influence on the Augustan poets

W. Robert Connor (U.S.), The fragments of Theopompus and the digression in Book X of the *Philippica*

Gilbert Lawall (U.S.), The pastoral poems of Theocritus

Michael C. Stokes (U.K.), The uses of the terms "one" and "many" in the pre-Socratic philosophers; a history of pre-Socratic cosmogony

Leonardo Tarán (Argentina), The *Epinomis*; Platonic philosophy

Erich Thummer (Austria), A commentary on the *Isthmian Odes* of Pindar

Anne-Marie Vérilhac (France), Funeral epigrams on young boys

1964–1965

Anne Amory (U.S.), The *Odyssey*, with particular attention to traditional epithets

Bernhard Kytzler (Germany), The Greek epistolographic tradition; an edition of the *Octavius*

Pierre Pachet (France), The technical vocabulary of the Stoic philosophy; an edition with a translation and a commentary on the fragments of Cleanthes

Carlo O. Pavese (Italy), The Sophoclean papyri; a new Oxyrhynchus papyrus of Pindar

Jan Pečírka (Czechoslovakia), Land ownership and citizen status in the Greek *polis*, with special attention to Athens

Gregory M. Sifakis (Greece), Prosopographical, epigraphical, and archeological problems of the history of the Hellenistic theater

William J. Slater (U.K.), A new Pindar lexicon

Peter Westervelt (U.S.), The similes of the *Iliad* and their role in the continuity of the poem

1965–1966

Alison M. Burford (U.K.), The social, economic, and cultural status of artists and craftsmen in ancient Greek society

Walter Burkert (Germany), Initiation rites in Greek cults and mythology

Eugen Dönt (Austria), The history of Platonism from Plato to Plotinus

Pierre Laurens (France), The relation of Martial to the Greek epigrammatic tradition

Anne Lebeck (U.S.), Theme and image in the *Oresteia* of Aeschylus

Harry M. Neumann (U.S.), Plato, with particular reference to the *Symposium*

Joseph A. Russo (U.S.), Homeric formula and meter

Ernst Sandvoss (Germany), The concepts of *soteria* and *diaphthora* in Plato's *Laws*

1966–1967

Klaus E.L. Bartels (Germany), Aristotelian zoology

Robert H. Drews (U.S.), Greek universal historians, with special attention to Ephorus

C. Thomas Gelzer (Switzerland), Neoplatonic allegorical literature and the text of Musaeus

Woldemar E.H. Görler (Germany), Antiochus of Ascalon and the Middle Academy

Nicolaos Hourmouziades (Greece), Mute figures in Greek drama

Donald Kagan (U.S.), Thucydides' account of the Peloponnesian War

David B. Robinson (U.K.), Platonic and Aristotelian ethics

Dirk M. Schenkeveld (Netherlands), The literary treatises of Dionysius of Halicarnassus

1967–1968

M. Rosemary Arundel (U.K.), An essay, text, and commentary on Empedocles

Douglas D. Feaver (U.S.), Greek music and instruments

Bettie Forte (U.S.), Greco-Roman relations from the fourth century B.C. through the second century A.D.

William W. Fortenbaugh (U.S.), Aristotle's conception of moral virtue

Herwig C. Görgemanns (Germany), Editions of Origenes' *De Principiis* and Plato's *Crito*

F. David Harvey (U.K.), Democratic ideals and concepts in Greek states during the fifth and fourth centuries B.C.

Gustav A. Seeck (Germany), Types of dramatic characters in Euripides

Charles P. Segal (U.S.), The Sophists and Democritus

1968–1969

J. Norman Austin (U.S.), The Homeric idea of poetics in the *Odyssey*

David J. Blackman (U.K.), Epigraphical documents relating to the history of the Athenian navy

David E. Hahm (U.S.), The physical theories of the Stoics

Alexander L.W. Kleinlogel (Germany), An edition of the scholia to Thucydides

Kjeld Matthiessen (Germany), An edition of the *Hecuba* of Euripides

Marsh H. McCall, Jr. (U.S.), An edition of the *Suppliants* of Aeschylus

Wesley D. Smith (U.S.), Early Greek medical theory

Krystyna Weyssenhoff (Poland), The correspondence of Alexander the Great

1969–1970

Jack M. Balcer (U.S.), Greek and Near Eastern history, with special attention to numismatic and epigraphical evidence

Malcolm S. Brown (U.S.), Plato and Greek mathematics

Diskin Clay (U.S.), Lucretius' knowledge of Epicurean philosophy

Walter Leszl (Italy), Aristotelian metaphysics

Gerhart Schneeweiss (Germany), Ethical concepts governing the composition of Plutarch's *Lives*

Kyriakos Tsantsanoglou (Greece), An edition of new fragments of ancient authors in the Salonica manuscript of Photius

John Vaio (U.S.), An edition of Babrius

Ingomar Weiler (Austria), The concept of the *Agon* in Greek mythology

1970–1971

O. Kimball Armayor (U.S.), Herodotus as an epic rather than a "scientific" historian

Gianfranco Fabiano (Italy), Literary studies on Theocritus

Irwin L. Merker (U.S.), A historical commentary on Diodorus, books 18 to 20

John Michael Moore (U.K.), A text of Polybius

Theodora H. Price (Greece), Greek hero cults, with special reference to the archeological evidence

Pietro Pucci (U.S.), An edition of the *Clouds* of Aristophanes; Euripidean tragedy

Oliver P. Taplin (U.K.), The dramatic technique of the Greek tragedians

Christian Wolff (U.S.), Literary studies in Euripides, particularly the *Helen*

1971–1972

Bruce Elliot Donovan (U.S.), The Euripidean papyri; a bibliography of literary papyri

Hermann Funke (Germany), Ancient allegorical interpretations of poetry

John Glucker (U.K.), Antiochus and the Late Academy

Sarah C. Humphreys (U.S.), Kinship in the Greek city-state

John David Moore (U.S.), An edition with commentary of Plato's *Symposium*

Jacques Peron (France), The techniques of Pindaric poetry

Franz Ferdinand Schwarz (Austria), A commentary on Arrian's *Indica*

Charlotte L. Stough (U.S.), Plato's metaphysics, with special attention to the *Phaedo* and *Parmenides*

1972–1973

Edwin L. Brown (U.S.), Astronomical sources of imagery in classical literature

Thomas Drew-Bear (U.S.), A history of Greco-Roman civilization in Phrygia

Michael Gagarin (U.S.), The political nature and background of Aeschylean tragedy

Wolfgang Dieter Lebek (Germany), Theophrastus' literary treatises and the linguistic and stylistic theories of the early Peripatetics

Jørgen Mejer (Denmark), The tradition of pre-Socratic philosophy from Plato to the end of antiquity

John J. Peradotto (U.S.), Myth and *Märchen* in the *Odyssey*: a study of the collision of conflicting narrative structures

Suzanne Roy-Saïd (France), The function of *nomos* in the *Oresteia*

Steven S. Tigner (U.S.), Physical dynamics in pre-Platonic cosmology

1973–1974

Gerald M. Browne (U.S.), An edition of the *Sortes Astrampsychi* for the *Bibliotheca Teubneriana*

Sylwester Dworacki (Poland), The dramatic technique of Menander

Staffan Fogelmark (Sweden), Homeric features in the poetry of Pindar and Bacchylides

Charles D. Hamilton (U.S.), The fourth-century orators, particularly Isocrates and Demosthenes

Alexander P.D. Mourelatos (U.S.), The philosophy of the early Greek Atomists

Bernd Seidensticker (Germany), Ancient tragicomedy

Daniel P. Tompkins (U.S.), Characterization, language, and historiography in Thucydides

Ronald A. Zirin (U.S.), Greek ideas about the nature of the sounds of human speech

1974–1975

Elizabeth Ann Fisher (U.S.), Greek knowledge of Latin literature in the Roman empire

Paul Siegfried Jäkel (Germany), The tragic poets, with particular attention to Euripidean tragic fragments

David Keyt (U.S.), Aristotle's political philosophy

Linda Collins Reilly (U.S.), Slavery in ancient Greece

Christopher Rowe (U.K.), Aristotle's *Politics*

Carl A. Rubino (U.S.), Cultural crisis and political language in fifth-century Greece

Peter Siewert (Germany), The literary testimonia for the Cerameicus; points of contact between tragedy and contemporary history

John Van Sickle (U.S.), Bucolic poetry as an ancient literary genre; the new Archilochus poem

1975–1976

Henry J. Blumenthal (U.K.), Neoplatonic commentators on Aristotle; Homeric linguistics

Frederick T. Griffiths (U.S.), The non-pastoral idylls of Theocritus

Michael W. Haslam (U.K.), The papyrus texts of the Greek tragedians

Louis Aryeh Kosman (U.S.), The importance of the dialogue form for an understanding of Platonic philosophy

Tomás Calvo Martínez (Spain), Models of language in Parmenides, Plato, and Aristotle

Hunter R. Rawlings III (U.S.), The structure of Thucydides' *History*

Thomas A. Szlezák (Switzerland), Platonic doctrines, written and unwritten

Nicholas P. White (U.S.), The ethics and moral psychology of the early and middle Stoics

1976–1977

Apostolos N. Athanassakis (U.S.), A philological commentary on *Iliad I*

Ann L.T. Bergren (U.S.), The poetics of epic verse

Deborah Boedeker (U.S.), Archaic Greek poetry

Penelope Bulloch (U.K.), An edition of Aristophanes' *Plutus*

John Patrick Lynch (U.S.), The history of the Platonic Academy and institutionalized higher education in Athens

Minor M. Markle III (U.S.), The history of the fourth century B.C., with special reference to Philip II of Macedon

Kurt A. Raaflaub (Switzerland), The idea of freedom in archaic and classical Greece

Susan Mary Sherwin-White (U.K.), Epigraphical and historical studies of Antiochus the Great

1977–1978

Lawrence J. Bliquez (U.S.), A new edition of Nachmanson's *Historische Attische Inscriften*

Denis J. Corish (Eire), The development of Greek theories of time

Daniel T. Devereux (U.S.), The doctrine of moral goodness in four early Platonic dialogues

William E. Higgins (U.S.), An intellectual and cultural history of *philotimia* in Greco-Roman antiquity

Jadwiga Kubinska (Poland), Epigraphical formulas for the protection of monuments in Greek inscriptions in Asia Minor

Volker Langholf (Germany), The investigative methods of the authors of the Hippocratic *Epidemiae*

Ian Mueller (U.S.), The philosophical presuppositions of Euclid's *Elements*

William C. Mullen (U.S.), Pindar's eleven odes for victors from Aegina

1978–1979

Liliane M.J.Gh. Bodson (Belgium), The place and function of animals in Greek society and religion

Jenny Strauss Clay (U.S.), Gods and men in the *Odyssey*

Antonios Kapsomenos (Greece), Tragic diction, with special emphasis on Aeschylus

Richard Patterson (U.S.), Plato's conception of the soul as self-moving motion

Peter J. Rhodes (U.K.), A commentary on the *Aristotelian Constitution of Athens*

James H. Tatum (U.S.), The *Cyropaedia* of Xenephon

Marc J.C. Waelkens (Belgium), Epigraphical and topographical studies of sarcophagi in Phrygia

Paul B. Woodruff (U.S.), Translation, and commentary on the *Hippias Major*

1979–1980

Polymnia Athanassiadi-Fowden (Greece), The last Neoplatonists and the problem of the persecution and martyrdom of pagans in the late Roman empire

Jon-Christian Billigmeier (U.S.), A comparative and historical grammar of Mycenean Greek

Susan G. Cole (U.S.), Epigraphical and historical studies centered on the mysteries of Dionysos

Allan Gotthelf (U.S.), Aristotle's conception of final causality

Augusto Guida (Italy), A new edition of the *Lexicon Vindobonense*

Andreas Katsouris (Cyprus), The technique of New Comedy

Mae J. Smethurst (U.S.), Greek tragedy and Japanese Noh plays

Donald Zeyl (Canada), Topics in the philosophy of Socrates (*akrasia*, hedonism, the unity of virtues)

1980–1981

Jan N. Bremmer (Netherlands), Birth, maturity, and death in classical Greece: a study of the rites of passage

Peter H. Burian (U.S.), Structure and convention in Greek tragedy

Maria Dzielska (Poland), The ancient evidence for the career and teachings of Apollonius of Tyana

Richard Kraut (U.S.), Moral expertise in the philosophy of Socrates

Paul A. Rahe (U.S.), The career of Lysander; Spartan society in the sixth and fifth centuries

Tessa Rajak (U.K.), The historian Flavius Josephus

Nicholas J. Richardson (U.K.), Ancient criticism and interpretation of the Homeric poems

Thomas Schwertfeger (Germany), Archaic Greek history

1981–1982

Walter Eder (Germany), Lawgivers in archaic Greece

Christoph Eucken (Germany), Isocrates, Plato, and Aristotle

Paul David Kovacs (U.S.), Euripides' *Heracles* and *Trojan Women*

Thomas R. Martin (U.S.), Demetrius Poliorcetes and the Greek mainland cities

Andrew M. Miller (U.S.), The Homeric hymn to Apollo
Deborah K. Modrak (U.S.), Aristotle's theory of perception
Nancy F. Rubin (U.S.), Homeric epic
Cynthia W. Shelmerdine (U.S.), A cultural study of Mycenean society

1982–1983

Waltraut Desch (Austria), The gods in Euripidean drama
Kathy H. Eden (U.S.), Legal procedure and tragic structure in Greek, Roman, and Renaissance tragedy
Thomas J. Figueira (U.S.), The Aeginetan odes of Pindar
Lawrence J. Jost (U.S.), Studies in Aristotle's *Nicomachean* and *Eudemian Ethics*
John N. Kazazis (Greece), Typical scenes in Apollonius Rhodius' *Argonautica*
Robert D. Lamberton (U.S.), Neoplatonic allegorizing interpretations of Homer
James H. Lesher (U.S.), The Homeric concept of knowledge
Charles M. Reed (U.S.), Maritime traders in the Hellenistic period

1983–1984

Julia E. Annas (U.K.), Aristotle's philosophical theory of perception
Glenn R. Bugh (U.S.), The Athenian cavalry as an aristocratic social institution
Anne Carson (Canada), The Greek concept of Eros
Albio C. Cassio (Italy), Greek dialects and ancient dialectological research
James G. Lennox (Canada), Aristotle's "philosophy of biology"
Alice Swift Riginos (U.S.), The contribution of Alexandrian scholars to the development of ancient biography
Deborah H. Roberts (U.S.), Closure and narrative structure in Greek tragedy
Peter M. Smith (U.S.), Concepts of time and justice in archaic Greek poetry

1984–1985

Peter Bing (U.S.), A commentary on Callimachus' *Hymn to Delos*
Dorothea Frede (U.S.), Heraclitean hedonism in Plato's *Philebus*
Kevin H. Lee (New Zealand), A critical edition of Euripides' *Heracles*

73

Mary M.A. Mackenzie (U.K.), A study of paradox in Greek thought

Sheila H. Murnaghan (U.S.), The hero in epic and tragedy, with particular reference to Aristotle's *Poetics*

Michael B. Poliakoff (U.S.), Combat sports in the ancient world

Frank E. Romer (U.S.), The idea of tyranny at Athens down to 336 B.C.

Simon R. Slings (Netherlands), A critical edition of Plato's eighth tetralogy

1985–1986

David Charles (U.K.), Aristotle's account of meaning and natural kinds

Robert Garland (U.K.), The history of the Piraeus

Anne H. Groton (U.S.), A commentary on Menander's *Aspis*

Arthur Madigan, S.J. (U.S.), A translation of Alexander of Aphrodisias' commentary on Aristotle's *Metaphysics Gamma*

Richard McKim (Canada), The role of Socrates in Plato's early and middle dialogues

Hanna M. Roisman (Israel), The word and idea of *kerdos* in Greek literature

Joseph Roisman (Israel), The communication of information in ancient Greece

Susan C. Shelmerdine (U.S.), A commentary on the *Homeric Hymn to Hermes*

Walter Stockert (Austria), A commentary on Euripides' *Iphigenia at Aulis*

1986–1987

Daniel R. Blickman (U.S.), The origins of Greek teleological ethics

R. Bracht Branham (U.S.), A literary study of Lucian's satires

Helena Cichocka (Poland), The rhetorical tradition of Hermogenes

Anthony T. Edwards (U.S.), The country and the city from Homer through the fourth century B.C.

Enrico Livrea (Italy), Nonnos' *Paraphrase of St. John's Gospel*

Robert J. Mondi (U.S.), Hesiod's use of mythic narratives

Georg Petzl (Germany), Inscriptions of Lydia and Commagene

John Walsh (U.S.), History of the Pentecontaëtia

Christopher K. Callanan (U.S.), Middle Platonic and Neoplatonic commentaries on Plato

Michael Erler (Germany), Epicurus and Epicureanism

André Laks (France), Plato's political philosophy

Adele C. Scafuro (U.S.), Herodotean influence on Hellenistic historiography

Theodore Scaltsas (Greece), An Aristotelian theory of substance

Pauline Schmitt-Pantel (France), "Histoire des Moeurs"

Niall W. Slater (U.S.), Theatrical self-consciousness in Aristophanes

Mark Toher (U.S.), Funeral laws in archaic Greek and Roman law codes

1988–1989

Osmund Bopearachchi (Sri Lanka), A numismatic and historical study of the Indo-Greeks

Thomas W. Gallant (U.S.), Household and community in ancient Greece

Henry Mendell (U.S.), Aristotle's philosophy of mathematics

Cynthia Patterson (U.S.), Patterns of membership in the *polis* before Aristotle

Hermann S. Schibli (Germany), The descent of the soul in pagan and Christian antiquity

David Shive (U.S.), The unity of authorship of the *Iliad* and *Odyssey*

Allan Silverman (U.S.), Plato on the separation of knowledge from belief

David Whitehead (U.K.), Aineias the Tactician: translation, introduction, commentary

1989–1990

Edwin M. Carawan (U.S.), Rhetoric and law in classical Athens

Andrew Ford (U.S.), Criticism of poetry in fifth-century Athens

Andrei Lebedev (U.S.S.R.), The transmission of Greek physical doxography

Maria Jagoda Luzzatto (Italy), Aesop and the Aesopic *logoi*

Ian Morris (U.K.), Economic growth and ideological change in Greek city-states

Josiah Ober (U.S.), Athenian critics of popular rule
Anthony W. Price (U.K.), Mental conflict; Aristotle's *Parva Naturalia*
Maurice P. Rehm (U.S.), Marriage and funeral rituals in Greek tragedy

1990–1991 (EXPECTED)

Patricia Kenig Curd (U.S.), The influence of Parmenides and Heraclitus on Plato

Eyjólfur Kjalar Emilsson (Iceland), Plotinus, *Ennead VI*, 4–5: English translation and commentary

Michael A. Flower (U.S.), Theopompus of Chios and fourth-century historiography

Geneviève Hoffmann (France), Maiden and woman in Athenian society

Steven H. Lonsdale (U.S.), Dance and ritual play in Greek religion

Irad Malkin (Israel), Myths and cults as validations of colonization

Emmanuel Voutiras (Greece), The cults of ancient Macedonia

Roslyn Weiss (U.S.), Impediments to the teachability of virtue in Plato

ENDNOTES

A NOTE ON SOURCES. This study is based largely on unpublished sources, only a few of which have made their way into libraries and archives; most are still to be found in current office files. The main sources are the office files of Paul Mellon in Washington, D.C., the office files of Old Dominion Foundation, which are retained by Old Dominion Foundation's successor, the Andrew W. Mellon Foundation in New York City, the papers of Nathan M. Pusey in the Harvard University Archives (quoted by permission of the Harvard University Archives), and the files of the Center for Hellenic Studies itself. I have benefited also from interviews with Thomas H. Beddall, Professor Bernard M.W. Knox, Director Emeritus of the Center for Hellenic Studies, and Nathan M. Pusey, President Emeritus of Harvard University.

Shortly after the center was established, Thomas Beddall collected many of the most important documents bearing on its origins (which exist generally in multiple copies) and assembled them into a volume which is retained in Mr. Mellon's office in Washington. For the sake of convenience, I have cited this collection (as Document A, B, etc.) whenever possible. Another important source is the minutes of the meetings of the committee for the humanities, which Mr. Beddall compiled, also still retained in Mr. Mellon's office. These are cited by their date.

1. William McGuire, *Bollingen: An Adventure in Collecting the Past* (Princeton, 1982); *Report of Old Dominion Foundation, Inc., 1941–1950*, 11; Old Dominion Foundation, *Report, 1941–1966*, 7.

2. Flexner to Huntington Cairns, 27 February 1953, Huntington Cairns Papers, container 10, "Flexner, Abraham, 1952–53," Manuscript Division, Library of Congress.

3. Howard Mumford Jones, *One Great Society: Humane Learning in the United States* (New York, 1959), 233, 237.

4. Abraham Flexner, *Abraham Flexner: An Autobiography* (2d ed., New York, 1960), 277.

5. *Addresses Delivered at the Dedication of the Center for Hellenic Studies* (Washington, D.C., 1963), 28.

6. Cairns to Sir Herbert Read, 27 April 1953, Cairns Papers, container 30, "Read, (Sir) Herbert, 1939, 1948–54."

7. Mellon to Griswold, n.d. (received 26 January 1953), A. Whitney Griswold Presidential Records, YRG 2-A-16, box 155, "Mellon, Paul (1950, 1951; 1954–1963)," Manuscripts and Archives, Yale University Library.

8. *Addresses Delivered at the Dedication of the Center*, 28.

9. Memorandum by Cairns, October 1954 (Document A); memorandum by Cairns, 9 June 1955 (Document B); Cairns to Mellon, 20 December 1956 (Document C).

10. [Cairns] to T. M. Knox (draft), 22 May 1956, "Residence in Aid of the Humanities: Mr. Barrett's Early Material," Old Dominion Foundation.

11. Cairns to Read, 9 February 1959, Cairns Papers, container 30, "Read, (Sir) Herbert, 1956–64."

12. Memorandum by Barzun ("Queries and Comments on Mr. Cairns's Memorandum of December 20, 1956"), 26 June 1959 (with Minutes, 26 June 1959).

13. Minutes, 1 September 1959.

14. Minutes, 9 December 1959.

15. Cairns to Read, 12 February 1959, Cairns Papers, container 30, "Read, (Sir) Herbert, 1956–64."

16. Memorandum by Mrs. Huntington Cairns ("The Residence"), February 1960 (Document DD).

17. Notes by Ernest Brooks, Jr., 29 December 1958, "Residence in Aid of the Humanities: Yellow Sheets," Old Dominion Foundation.

18. Minutes, 14 May 1959.

19. Beddall to Brooks, 16 September 1958, "Residence in Aid of the Humanities," Old Dominion Foundation.

20. Memorandum by R. Keith Kane for Nathan M. Pusey et al., 8 December 1958, Papers of Nathan M. Pusey, UAI.5.169, box 14, "Center for Hellenic Studies," Harvard University Archives; Kane to Pusey, 7 January 1960, Pusey Papers, box 157, "Old Dominion Foundation."

21. Mellon to Griswold, 18 December 1956, Griswold Papers, box 155, "Mellon, Paul (1950; 1951; 1954–1963)."

22. Minutes of the finance committee, 6 June 1955, Old Dominion Foundation.

23. Marie Beale, *Decatur House and Its Inhabitants* (Washington, D.C., 1954), chaps. 11, 12.

24. Mrs. Beale to Cairns, 2 March 1950, Cairns Papers, container 2, "Beale, Mrs. Truxton."

25. Memorandum by Cairns, 9 June 1955 (Document B).

26. Notes by Brooks (?) ("Phone from H.C."), 14 June 1955, "Residence in Aid of the Humanities: Expenses," Old Dominion Foundation.

27. These negotiations and transactions can be followed in "Residence in Aid of the Humanities: Property," Old Dominion Foundation.

28. Last will and testament of Marie Beale, 10 May 1956, item IV (a).

29. Minutes of the finance committee, 8 October 1956, Old Dominion Foundation.

30. Cairns to John D. Barrett, 14 November 1956, "Residence in Aid of the Humanities: Mr. Barrett's Early Material," Old Dominion Foundation.

31. Items IV (b), XVI (bb).

32. Minutes, 30 September 1958.

33. American Security and Trust Company et al. *v.* President and Fellows of Harvard College et al., no. 1379-57, slip op (D.D.C., 12 May 1958) (I wish to thank Yvonne Facchina of Sullivan & Cromwell for help with this reference); memorandum from Kelley, Drye, Newhall and Maginnes, 17 June 1958, "Contributions Made: Residence in Aid of the Humanities," Old Dominion Foundation; James C. Rogers to Edward K. Bachman, 22 April 1958, "Residence in Aid of the Humanities: Property," Old Dominion Foundation.

34. Memorandum by Charles D. Dickey, 26 June 1958, "Residence in Aid of the Humanities: Property," Old Dominion Foundation.

35. Minutes, 24 April 1959.

36. Minutes, 9 December 1959.

37. Minutes of the finance committee, 14 May 1956, Old Dominion Foundation.

38. Memorandum by Ezekial G. Stoddard ("Compliance with Conditions Covering Devise of Whitehaven Property in Beale Will"), 11 September 1958, "Residence in Aid of the Humanities: Deeds, Wills, Title Insurance, Etc.," Old Dominion Foundation.

39. Notes ("8/7/58, Mtg with PM, S. Stevens, T. Beddall"), "Residence in Aid of the Humanities: Property," Old Dominion Foundation.

40. Author's interviews with Beddall, 24 September 1987, and Pusey, 4 March 1988, both stressed Stevens's dominant role.

41. Mellon to Schmidt, 18 August 1958; Mellon to Cairns, 26 August 1958, "Residence in Aid of the Humanities: Letters—Members of Committee," Old Dominion Foundation.

42. Minutes, 30 September 1958.

43. Ibid.

44. Memorandum by Cairns, 17 November 1959 (with Minutes, 9 December 1959).

45. Stevens to Schmidt, 28 November 1958 (Document F).

46. Minutes, 30 September 1958.

47. Minutes, 14 May 1959; 9 December 1959.

48. Minutes, 9 December 1959.

49. Stevens to Mellon, 1 October 1958, "Old Dominion Foundation: Center for Hellenic Studies (1952–1959) PM," office of Paul Mellon.

50. Stevens to Beddall, 21 July 1958, "Center for Hellenic Studies, 1958 (THB)," office of Paul Mellon.

51. Minutes, 6 September 1958.

52. Minutes, 19 November 1958; notes ("11/19/58, Dr. Pusey"), "Residence in Aid of the Humanities: Yellow Sheets," Old Dominion Foundation.

53. Kirk to Stevens, 5 November 1958 (with Minutes, 19 November 1958).

54. Minutes, 29 December 1959.

55. Minutes, 29 December 1958; notes ("EB Notes, Meeting in

Princeton, 12/29/58"), "Residence in Aid of the Humanities: Yellow Sheets," Old Dominion Foundation.

56. Minutes, 19 February 1959.

57. Memorandum by Beddall ("Residence or Institute for the Humanities"), 6 January 1959 (Document L).

58. Minutes, 26 June 1959.

59. Minutes, 24 April 1959.

60. Minutes, 19 February 1959; 24 April 1959.

61. Minutes, 9 December 1959; Stevens to Beddall, 31 December 1958 (with Minutes, 29 December 1958).

62. Minutes, 30 September 1958.

63. Memorandum by Stevens for Barrett et al., 8 December 1958 (Document G).

64. Memorandum by Kane for Pusey et al., 8 December 1958; memorandum by Kane for Pusey et al., 2 January 1959, Pusey Papers, box 14, "Center for Hellenic Studies."

65. Kane to Stevens, 19 February 1959 (Document S).

66. Pusey to Brooks, 19 February 1959; "The Institute of Hellenic and Humanistic Studies" (Document T).

67. Bradley to O. M. Shaw, 4 February 1959 (Document O).

68. Kane to Stevens, 19 February 1959 (Document S).

69. Paul Buck to Pusey, 13 February 1959, Pusey Papers, box 14, "Center for Hellenic Studies."

70. Memorandum by Kracauer ("The Residence"), July 1959 (Document Y).

71. Barzun to Brooks, 14 July 1959 (Document X).

72. Minutes, 24 April 1959.

73. Memorandum by Stevens for Barrett et al., 8 December 1958 (Document G).

74. Minutes, 24 April 1959.

75. Notes, [24 April 1959], "Harvard University: Center for Hellenic Studies: Miscellaneous," Old Dominion Foundation. See Minutes, 14 May 1959.

76. Minutes, 21 October 1959.

77. Minutes, 26 June 1959; 1 September 1959; notes ("Mtg 9/1/59, J. Barzun"), "Residence in Aid of the Humanities: Yellow Sheets," Old Dominion Foundation; memorandum by Barzun ("Queries and Comments"), 26 June 1959 (with Minutes, 26 June 1959); Barzun to Brooks, 14 July 1959 (Document X).

78. Thacher to Cairns, 12 February 1959 (Document P); Cairns to Barrett, 17 February 1959 (Document R); Clagett to Cairns, 24 March 1959 (Document W).

79. Memorandum by Mathews ("Report on the Residence"), 25 February 1959 (Document U).

80. Cairns to Barrett, 17 February 1959 (Document R).

81. Minutes, 14 May 1959.

82. Memorandum by Cairns, 17 November 1959 (with Minutes, 9 December 1959).

83. Minutes, 9 December 1959.

84. Memorandum by Cairns, 23 December 1959 (Document CC).

85. Memorandum by Mathews, 4 January 1960; memorandum by Kracauer, n.d., "Residence in Aid of the Humanities: Reports," Old Dominion Foundation.

86. Minutes, 28 January 1960.

87. Memorandum by Mrs. Huntington Cairns ("The Residence"), February 1960 (Document DD); "Residence in Aid of the Humanities: Mrs. Cairns—Memoranda and Notes," Old Dominion Foundation.

88. Memorandum by Stevens for Mellon et al., 23 July 1959 (Document Z).

89. See Stevens to Brooks, 30 September 1959, "Residence in Aid of the Humanities: Material from Harvard and Dr. Pusey," Old Dominion Foundation.

90. Memorandum by Kane for Pusey, 26 July 1959, Pusey Papers, box 157, "Old Dominion Foundation."

91. Memorandum by Stevens for Mellon et al., 23 July 1959 (Document Z).

92. Memorandum by Pusey for Stevens, 25 September 1959 (Document BB).

93. Crane Brinton, ed., *The Society of Fellows* (Cambridge, 1959).

94. Kane to Pusey, 31 December 1959, Pusey Papers, box 157, "Old Dominion Foundation."

95. Ibid.

96. Memorandum by William Bentinck-Smith for Pusey, 31 March 1960, Pusey Papers, box 157, "Old Dominion Foundation."

97. Kane to Pusey, 7 January 1960, Pusey Papers, box 157, "Old Dominion Foundation."

98. Ibid.

99. Memorandum by Kane ("Memorandum of Conversation with and between Messrs. Nathan Pusey, Stoddard Stevens and R. Keith Kane on April 21, 1960, at Mr. Stevens' Office"), 21 April 1960, Pusey Papers, box 157, "Old Dominion Foundation."

100. Ibid.

101. Minutes, 20 May 1960.

102. Memorandum by Kane for Pusey, 20 May 1960; Kane to Pusey, 25 May 1960, Pusey Papers, box 157, "Old Dominion Foundation."

103. Author's interview with Pusey, 4 March 1988.

104. Minutes, 8 October 1960.

105. Memorandum by Kane for Pusey, 20 October 1960, Pusey Papers, box 187, "Old Dominion Foundation."

106. Minutes of Old Dominion Foundation, 7 December 1960, Old Dominion Foundation.

107. *The Washington Post*, 6 January 1961.

108. Vermeule to Elder, 8 February 1961, "Other Applications: Dean Elder, 1961," Center for Hellenic Studies.

109. Blanding to Pusey, 23 January 1961, "Harvard University: Center for Hellenic Studies: Letters of Congratulation," Old Dominion Foundation.

110. "Harvard University: Center for Hellenic Studies," Old Dominion Foundation.

111. "Harvard University: Center for Hellenic Studies: Letters re Sale of Property," Old Dominion Foundation.

112. Kane to Pusey, 10 November 1960; Oates to Pusey, 15 No-

vember 1960, Pusey Papers, box 187, "Old Dominion Foundation."

113. Mellon to Griswold, 30 December 1960, "Harvard University: Center for Hellenic Studies," Old Dominion Foundation.

114. *Yale Daily News*, 5 April 1961.

115. Pusey to Brooks, 13 December 1960, "Harvard University: Center for Hellenic Studies," Old Dominion Foundation.

116. Putnam to Knox, 7 August 1961, "Knox, Bernard M.W., 1961–62," Center for Hellenic Studies.

117. "Center for Hellenic Studies: Publicity: Dean Elder, 1961," Center for Hellenic Studies.

118. Minutes of the administrative committee, 20 April 1961, "Administrative Committee, 1961–62," Center for Hellenic Studies.

119. Ibid.

120. Knox to Kane, 8 May 1961, "CHS Center Building," Center for Hellenic Studies; Elder to members of the administrative committee, 9 May 1961, "Administrative Committee, 1961–62," Center for Hellenic Studies.

121. Kane to Knox, 17 July 1961, "CHS Center Buildings," Center for Hellenic Studies.

122. Kane to members of the administrative committee et al., 21 July 1961, "Administrative Committee: Mr. Keith Kane—1961–62," Center for Hellenic Studies.

123. Kane to members of the administrative committee, 14 September 1961, "CHS Center Buildings," Center for Hellenic Studies.

124. Cross to Knox, 16 October 1961, "Architect: Mr. Page Cross, 1961–62," Center for Hellenic Studies.

125. Cross to Knox, 19 February 1962, "Cross & Son, Architect: Mr. Page Cross," Center for Hellenic Studies.

126. Cross to Knox, 6 March 1962, "Architect: Mr. Page Cross, 1961–62," Center for Hellenic Studies.

127. Minutes of the administrative committee, 18 December 1962, "Administrative Committee, 1962–63," Center for Hellenic Studies.

128. "Harvard University: Center for Hellenic Studies," Old Dominion Foundation.

129. "The 1989 Thomas Jefferson Medalist in Architecture: Paul Mellon," *Colonnade: The Newsjournal of the University of Virginia School of Architecture*, IV, no. 2 (Summer–Autumn 1989), 17.

130. Putnam to Knox, 26 September 1961; 23 October 1961, "Knox, Bernard M.W. Knox, 1961–62," Center for Hellenic Studies.

131. Knox, "The Center for Hellenic Studies and its Library," *Harvard Library Bulletin*, XIX (1971), 246.

132. Author's interview with Knox, 7 June 1988.

133. Putnam to the managing director, B.H. Blackwell, Ltd., 12 April 1961, "Knox, Bernard M.W., 1961–62," Center for Hellenic Studies.

134. Minutes of the administrative committee, 20 January 1962, "Administrative Committee, 1961–62," Center for Hellenic Studies.

135. Knox, "Center for Hellenic Studies and its Library," 249.

136. *Addresses Delivered at the Dedication of the Center*, 21-2, 38.

137. Annual report of the Center for Hellenic Studies, 1965–1966.

138. Knox to Sterling Dow, 14 December 1962, "Visiting Scholars, 1962–63," Center for Hellenic Studies.

139. Memorandum by Pusey, 20 May 1960 (with Minutes, 20 May 1960); "Harvard University: Center for Hellenic Studies: Press Release and News Clippings," Old Dominion Foundation.

140. Glen W. Bowersock, Walter Burkert, and Michael C.J. Putnam, eds., *Arktouros: Hellenic Studies Presented to Bernard M.W. Knox on the Occasion of His 65th Birthday* (Berlin and New York, 1979), vii.

PHOTOGRAPHIC CREDITS

Paul Mellon: Photograph by Horst; courtesy VOGUE. Copyright © by The Condé Nast Publications Inc.

Huntington Cairns: Courtesy of the Gallery Archives, National Gallery of Art.

Marie Beale: Courtesy of Decatur House. Decatur House is a museum property of the National Trust for Historic Preservation.

Whitehaven Street: Photograph by Aeroservices; courtesy of the Historical Society of Washington, D.C.

Stoddard M. Stevens: Courtesy of Sullivan & Cromwell.

Nathan M. Pusey: Photograph by Bachrach; courtesy of the Harvard University Archives.

R. Keith Kane: Photograph by Bachrach; courtesy of the Harvard University Archives.

Bernard M.W. Knox: Courtesy of Bernard M.W. Knox.

Fellows' houses under construction: Photograph by Stewart Bros. Photographers Inc.; courtesy of the Center for Hellenic Studies.

The administration building before it was painted white: Photograph by Stewart Bros. Photographers Inc.; courtesy of the Center for Hellenic Studies.

Nathan Pusey speaking: Courtesy of the Center for Hellenic Studies.

Paul Mellon speaking: Courtesy of the Center for Hellenic Studies.

Bernard Knox speaking: Courtesy of the Center for Hellenic Studies.

Archibald MacLeish and Paul Mellon: Courtesy of the Center for Hellenic Studies.

Guests with fellows' houses: Courtesy of the Center for Hellenic Studies.

87

Guests with the director's residence: Courtesy of the Center for Hellenic Studies.

John Finley visiting with family of Masaaki Kubo: Courtesy of the Center for Hellenic Studies.

Bernard Knox with visitor in front of the "bachelors' quarters": Courtesy of the Center for Hellenic Studies.

Administration building as it appears today: Courtesy of the Center for Hellenic Studies.